'I ⸳⸳⸳eously written. On more than
one occasion it made me well up . . . most certainly
not just for the fan club' *Guardian*

'Beautifully crafted and brilliantly well-written . . .
his memoir is a thought-provoking meditation on how
our childhoods form the people we become, as well as a
love letter to London . . . The book is perfect as it is, but
there's no question that we need a second volume'
Anna van Praagh, *Evening Standard*

'A thrillingly energetic, bracingly entertaining
snapshot of a writer hitting his first full flush, leaving you
wishing two things. One: that you'd formed a band. Two:
that he changes his mind about documenting the coke-
blurred mornings to come' *Record Collector*

'An ineffably romantic coming-of-age story; a beautiful
reminder of the magic that happens round the edges'
Sunday Times

'His memoir is melancholy and evocative, a
dreamy ballad recalling the time before the drugs
and the band break-up' *Sunday Express*

COAL BLACK
MORNINGS

BRETT ANDERSON

(ABACUS)

ABACUS

First published in Great Britain in 2018 by Little, Brown
This paperback edition published in 2019 by Abacus

13 5 7 9 10 8 6 4 2

A CIP catalogue record for this book
is available from the British Library.

ISBN 978-1-4087-1048-7

Typeset in Granjon by M Rules
Printed and bound in Great Britain by
Clays Ltd, Elcograf S.p.A.

Papers used by Abacus are from well-managed forests
and other responsible sources.

Abacus
An imprint of
Little, Brown Book Group
Carmelite House
50 Victoria Embankment
London EC4Y 0DZ

An Hachette UK Company
www.hachette.co.uk

www.littlebrown.co.uk

For Lucian

COAL BLACK MORNINGS

FOREWORD

This is a book about failure. It's a book about poverty and family and friendship and the scruffy wonders of youth and, inevitably, it's a book about love and it's a book about loss. The very last thing I wanted to write was the usual 'coke and gold discs' memoir with which we've all become so familiar so any success in the story is implied. I've limited this strictly to the early years, before anyone really knew or really cared, and so the decision to end it at the point where I have, when we were all still starry-eyed and guileless, was utterly vital in order to achieve any sense of tone. I've always loved art and artists that find a place and have the discipline to stay in it; from *Never Mind The Bollocks* to *Music For Airports*, from Bruegel to Warhol, I've never seen repetition of themes as being a weakness, merely as essential in establishing identity. Anyway, the bloody-mindedness quite appeals to me. To stray beyond and to keep my voice fresh and void of cliché would have been impossible, and right now I have no desire to rake over those days again.

This then is a kind of prehistory; when all that I can bring to the second half of the story is a fresh perspective, here I am hopefully unearthing something new, hunched over the fossils of my past as it were. But sometimes it seems, looking back can be just as valuable as looking forward – learning from the person you were, often in the sense of how not to do things, but occasionally glimpsing those moments of wonder to which youth alone is often privy. For years I avoided writing anything, preferring the veil of silence and mystery to the inherent sense of exhibitionism contained within any such process, but for some reason I now feel an urgent need to impart. I suppose I have come to a stage in my life where I want to try to come to terms with who I am, and exploring my past on my own terms like this is a way to try to achieve that.

It's interesting how writing it has made me ponder the broader concept of truth. Regardless of how valiantly you try to be faithful to the facts it will always only be from one point of view. Fascinatingly, though, others around you might see things differently or even see things the same way but choose to interpret them differently, so it's important to understand that there is no such thing as absolute truth, just perspectives. Certainly, writing it has been a wrenching experience, and revisiting those distant corridors has at each point plunged me magically back, reliving the feelings: the breathless shivers of love, the crushing pain of loss and death, and forming the words for some of the chapters has been hard and at times pushed me to tears. Reading it through, there are moments where I come across as mawkish and cloying, or clingy and weak, and I see myself for the sometimes callow, anxious soul that I probably was and possibly still sometimes am, but I think at least it's honest. We stumble through life leaving an embarrassing, sticky trail, and it's often only at times of reflection like this that we realise quite what a mess we sometimes made.

There are things about ushering this out into the world that scare me, of course. I can't say I'm looking forward to any gossip that might follow, and there's a natural fear when you expose yourself so nakedly, but effectively I've been doing that for years. Strangely, I am less concerned about the reaction from those who have read this than the reaction from those who haven't; it's the misleading, ill-informed assumptions that I'm slightly dreading. I've learned over the years that no matter how carefully you tread around some subjects they will always push their way to the front like bullies and hog the headlines, denying the finer points the oxygen of publicity. It's this disparity that I suppose I will have to accept with good grace as just an unfortunate part of the process. Given these misgivings, you might ask yourself why I'm bothering, and I have asked myself the same question many times, but if you will bear with me I will be wending my way towards some sort of explanation. It has, of course, stirred up feelings that I have denied myself for years and has inevitably fed into my current thread of song-writing, and for that alone it has been worth it. The last two albums I have written have both been very much about family and the sense of lineage with which parenthood imbues you, and those ruminations have led me to want to take this process to the obvious conclusion. At the time of writing this, I have no book deal and no real knowledge whether anyone will be particularly interested in publishing this as it is. There's an old musician's interview cliché that worthy but unimaginative band members trot out about how they just make music for themselves and if anyone else is interested then that's just a bonus. I'll adapt that by saying that I'm writing this specifically for one person – my son – and if anyone else is interested then *that's* a bonus. When he's old enough, which may indeed be when I am no longer around, at least he'll have this to add a little bit of truth to the story of who his dad was and the passions and privations he lived through, and ultimately where we both came from. I think about my own father a lot, and now that he's gone often mull over the real person he was; teasing out little fragments of memory and picking out the bones of truth from the carcass of characterisation for which I'm probably slightly guilty. If I had a document like this to read about him and his life, I would treasure it, so hopefully when my son is curious and eventually ready, he might one day pick this up and know that his father loved and lost and fought and felt, and hopefully that will mean something to him.

1

I was born just after the first Summer of Love in the very room in which my father died thirty-eight years later. It was my parents' bedroom. She was a would-be painter who made money sewing underpriced dresses for local, well-heeled but parsimonious ladies, and he was a postman at the time, later to become a swimming pool attendant, ice-cream man, window cleaner and eventually a taxi driver. Theirs was a world of lino and pregnancy tests, hired furniture and rent collectors; a country mile from the swinging sixties Carnaby Street cliché, and more akin to the joyless grey of post-war Britain than the popular Technicolor myth. The room was in one of those poky, claustrophobic, low-rise council houses – you know the type; they pepper the tatty parts of suburbia and the nation's drab dormitory towns, cramped and pebble-dashed, exiled to the outskirts, ignored and forever driven by.

Ours was the house right at the edge of the estate in a place called Lindfield, a village perched just outside and swallowed up by Haywards Heath; an anonymous commuter town, a drab, dreary little train stop somewhere between London and Brighton. It was a place where, beyond the torrid kitchen-sink dramas of everyday lower-middle-class life, nothing ever really happened and probably nothing ever really will.

My parents chose the house because they thought it would be nice to raise their kids next to a wood, as indeed it was but a few yards away beyond a graffitied, corrugated iron fence, and sat like a threat at the bottom of the concrete road was the local tip. At the weekend people would turn up to throw away their broken appliances and household detritus. It was a sea of rust and white enamel, a tangle of discarded furniture and springs and perished tyres and dried-up paint pots. To the local kids it was, of course, a wonderful and frightening playground, a source of constant fascination and danger. We would clamber over the rubble and mess around with the smashed-up mopeds and seized-up bicycle chains, unaware of the lurking dangers as we played in the skips with mercury from broken thermometers. Once, a small scuppered rowing boat appeared and became the centrepiece of our fevered games for a whole summer, until it was eventually vandalised and left to the cruel entropy of the elements. The area is a nature reserve now, and I sometimes wonder if the dog walkers and picnicking ramblers know about the rusting grave-yard beneath their Wellingtoned feet.

The house was small. Very small. Before my father died, I would return there for dutiful Christmas visits and would always be shocked by its almost toy-like scale. I had a sister, too, the lovely Blandine, named after the daughter of the Romantic Hungarian composer Franz Liszt. My dad, Peter, had named my sister, so it was thankfully left up to Sandra, my mum, to name me. For this I'm eternally grateful, as due to either coincidence or judgement I was born on the very date of Horatio Nelson's birthday, one of my father's heroes and a key member of his 'Big

Three' – an exclusive private club of idols that also housed Winston Churchill and the aforementioned Liszt. In later years, I remember my dad buying an enormous naval ensign Union Jack flag, which was almost as big as the house, and hoisting it up a makeshift flag-pole fixed to the wall of our tiny council house on each of their birthdays. Family lore tells me that terrifyingly I was millimetres away from being named Horatio but, according to my father, my mother named me after the actor Jeremy Brett, with some mutterings that it was also a nod to Roger Moore's character, Lord Brett Sinclair, from *The Persuaders* – perhaps some subconscious harbinger for future events.

So there were four of us cramped within the brick and breeze-block rooms of this cheap little chip-board house: Blandine, in her dank north-facing bedroom; my mum and dad, penned into their cramped conjugal enclave; and me, perched at the edge of the house in a sunny box-room just about large enough to contain my child's single bed and a few threadbare toys – a knitted woollen guardsman called Soldier, a grey mouse called Mouse and a horrible furry thing that I used to put up my nose called Tivvy, which my parents had got from some offer in the *TV Times*. My art college-educated mother painted clouds on the ceiling of my room, and I would lie there gazing at them, listening to the gentle sough of the traffic outside while my parents' rows erupted and stormed a few feet away in the next room.

I was a nervous, twitchy, anxious child, prone to bouts of insomnia and lonely, terrified hours awake staring at the grotesque faces that the folds at the top of the curtains seemed to make. Once the sun rose, I would wait for everyone else to wake up, staring for ages from my window at a pair of trees growing near the abandoned mushroom factory at the bottom of our road. One I called The Mouse and the other I called The Clown, and I would gaze transfixed as they swayed and billowed, seemingly locked in their immutable dispute, buoyed and buffeted by the eddies and currents of the high wind.

In many ways my upbringing was extremely normal, but at the same time strangely atypical in a way as I felt like we never really fitted in. Officially we lived in a quaint Sussex village but our house was somewhere the tourists never visited; nestled in a scruffy estate on the outskirts and hidden well away from the chocolate-box fantasy world of the high street. We were dirt poor, existing in penury in a cheap council house, but my parents filled it with trappings more akin to the lives of upper-middle-class Hampstead intellectuals. Mum's paintings were everywhere; she devoted her entire modest career to detailing the gently rolling Sussex countryside, and the walls would be full of her beautiful watercolour landscapes and intricately observed natural studies. Where her own work was absent she hung prints of Hendrick Avercamp, Vincent Van Gogh and Aubrey Beardsley. She had decorated the whole place with strong colours – midnight blues, William Morris wallpapers and her own rich velvet homemade curtains in the windows. And everywhere, of course, was the deafening torrent of my father's classical music: Wagner, Berlioz, Elgar, Chopin and the ubiquitous, inescapable Liszt. My own musical education must have been formed in this turbulent crucible, forged by the *Ring* Cycle and *Hungarian Rhapsody*, hammered into shape like Brünnhilde's breastplate by dark brooding musical landscapes and towering epic melodies. My dad would stand there wearing his slippers, his skinny little hairy legs poking out of his red silk dressing-gown, 'conducting' with his baton, lost in a delicious solipsism while his old Phillips reel-to-reel spooled on and on and the rest of us sat cowed and mute in the kitchen.

His was an obsession to end obsessions; he talked about Liszt in reverential, quasi-religious tones and even flirted with the idea of 'taking his minor orders' in homage to Liszt's later journey of faith – a preposterous idea given his status as a confirmed atheist. He was once called up for jury service, and after a two-week hiatus returned to reveal that when asked to swear on the Bible he had refused and demanded instead to do so on a biography of Franz Liszt; something, he said, he really believed in.

In the black and white years of the sixties he cruised around Haywards Heath on an old BSA bike with a sidecar clamped on, in which my mother would anxiously crouch and perch, fearful of any damage to her hair-do. As the family grew he acquired a three-wheeled Robin Reliant, the Sinclair C5 of its day, drivable with a motorcycle licence: a brittle fibreglass shell on wheels offering nominal protection and little dignity. By the time I arrived he drove us all around in a tatty, racing-green Morris Traveller, which was so decrepit that in September little mushrooms would grow from the rotten wooden side-frames. My sister and I would rattle around, seatbelt-less on the back seat, singing Abba songs. The car would vibrate worryingly when we drove at any speed on the motor-way, and if you looked closely you could see the road rushing by through little fissures in the floor pan. Unbelievably, every couple of years my father would manage to drive it all the way to Raiding in Austria on a pilgrimage to Liszt's birthplace, where he would take a small sample of soil from the ground to wear in a phial around his neck.

Living under my father's roof involved picking your way through a complex wilderness of seemingly pointless rules. He once wryly described his only indulgences in life as being 'an ounce of tobacco and a copy of the *Radio Times*', which he would jealously guard with a Gollum-like grip. Woe betide anyone who removed it from its special tartan holder, or got to it before he could schedule his listening pleasure with a series of Biroed circles, or even more transgressively took it from its home under the small wickerwork stool where he liked to place his feet while puffing and wheezing endlessly on his ever-present briar pipe. There were other rules about the proper time to eat plums and the 'correct' way to tie a tie, which on reflection don't quite translate, but at the time seemed narrow and petty, always betraying a sense that he was desperately trying to wrest control over the moving pieces of his world.

He was born into a military family and brought up in a depressing Haywards Heath council estate called Bentswood: an enclave of identical, boxy, nineteen thirties houses cloyed with alcoholism and violence and failure, the smell of stale sherry and dog food and the wintery fug of three-bar fires. My grandparents' house was littered with military memorabilia like Kukri knives, ornamental ammunition shells and trinkets from India where their family had been stationed for the first few years of my father's life. His mother was a frail, high-cheek-boned, bird-like woman, timid and browbeaten, and her husband, my dad's own father, was an abusive, hard-drinking soldier who seemed to care for little else but Khan, his enormous black Labrador, and who eventually threw his own son out of the house because Peter finally managed to stand up to him, unable to inure himself to the storm of invidious drunken brutality with which my grandfather ruled his pebble-dashed fiefdom. This upbringing left my dad with a legacy of absolute physical pacifism towards me, but in his murkier moments Larkin's gloomy prophecy of familial inheritance expressed itself in subtler ways. The dank claustrophobia of our doll's house was often paralleled by my father's capricious moods – the charming, crumpled eccentric supplanted by a brooding bully, the climate thick with tension and threat. His was a generation that simply wasn't given the tools to control and address its inner ghosts. My father's black dog slowly gnawed away and eventually killed him; a pernicious chain of events leading him towards isolation and depression and haemorrhage.

I must have some distant Scottish heritage, obviously, because of our surname, but also because my grandfather was a drummer and bagpipe player in the marching band of the Royal Scots Fusiliers. He was a distant, formal-looking, old-fashioned sort of man with combed-back, oily, Macassared hair and a ravaged drinker's face, who bizarrely was one of the few people you will ever hear about who died twice. After a series of unforgivable violent, drunken episodes his marriage finally crumbled and he staggered off to stay with old army friends or sleep at doss houses. The truth is sketchy but he seems to have drifted into a cycle of homelessness and extreme alcoholism, so no one was surprised when sometime in the nineties, after a long period of estrangement and rumours of nights spent on park benches, we were told that he had died – news to which my father seemed to react with a strange indifference. At least ten years later, however, he received a phone call from some institution asking if he would contribute to his father's funeral. It transpired that he had actually been alive all that time: drifting and drinking and spiralling further downwards. My dad was never able to forgive him for his reign of domestic terror and harboured such bitter hatred towards him that, despite the shock, he refused to contribute.

Although he never physically harmed me, my dad's brooding rages were terrifying and have probably left me with my own legacy of neurosis. He could be very controlling – always demanding to know where you were going if you left the room. To this day it's impossible for me to even go for a piss without telling my wife. It's like that scene in *The Shawshank Redemption* when Morgan Freeman's character gets the job as a bag-packer in the supermarket. At other times he could be hugely confrontational and would make outrageous or quixotic statements about politics and music. When I eventually drifted towards adolescence and began to challenge him, we would continually clash in increasingly bitter, cyclical debates over the relative merits of pop and classical. Christmas after Christmas would end in fraught, charged arguments as we sat glumly at the table in paper hats while he passionately but pointlessly tried to prove to me that the *Pathétique* was 'better' than 'Satisfaction'. The experience made me highly opinionated about music and probably prepared me wonderfully for a lifetime of over-explaining my own.

There were lighter moments, of course, too. He could be gentle and kind, and sweet and funny and wonderfully anti-materialistic, completely unaffected by the eighties climate of crushing ambition, content within his tiny kingdom of chip-board and paint. He was surprisingly practical, and was always sawing and drilling and gluing and hammering and fixing things with his perfectly maintained collection of tools. He made furniture and shelves and picture frames for my mother's paintings, and even his own speaker cabinets. One Easter holiday he was working away on what he told Blandine and me was a cabinet for his tools. We were puzzled by its need for chicken wire until on Easter day we were ushered out to the garden to be presented with a beautiful white rabbit each. He'd been building a hutch for them.

The rabbits became a looming presence in our little world. Every morning we would traipse over to the wasteland behind the dump by our house, and pick them dandelions and choice greenery, and our mum would make them a delicious-smelling, warm, mashed-up mealy thing in the winter made of oats and potato skins. Blandine even started what she called The Rabbit Club, the point of which was vague. The only rules of membership seemed to be that as a form of recognition between the members (just two – her and me) we would twitch our noses at each other. Anyone who knows me well will know that it's a habit I've found hard to shake.

If my father's obsession was Lizst, my sister's was *Watership Down*. She read her paperback version so often that the cover disintegrated, and she made her own replacement one with a lace and denim trim, and her own watercoloured interpretations of Hazel and Fiver et al. She was so keen for me to know the story that she actually paid me 2p an hour to listen to her read it aloud – a practice that later fed into other authors like Tolkien and Rosemary Sutcliffe. I don't ever remember being read cutesy young kids' books, though, and one of my earliest memories is of my mother reading me *Beowulf*. Blandine's influence on me was huge: she introduced me to literature, inspired me to want to be educated, and later played me the pop music of the sixties and seventies, which would grow and evolve within me and form the second strand of my musical self.

When I was about six or seven, Blandine and I started going to Sunday School. It was a white-brick, single-storey building on the edge of our estate run by a frail elderly couple called Mr and Mrs Marsh (my sister always joked that they should have lived somewhere called *Bog Cottage*). Anyway, I was far too young to understand any of the real spiritual dimensions of what I was signing up for, and looking back I'd have to interpret the whole experience as a process of indoctrination to which my atheist parents seemed blithely passive. I suppose what attracted me was the end-of-year 'prize-giving' ceremony where the children were rewarded for the number of days they had attended over the year. Depending on how many weekly stamps you had accrued, you would be presented with some childish bauble or book. Of course, the more ruthless local kids would exploit this and turn up just for that day, marching home triumphantly brandishing dot-to-dot books or bits of similarly worthless religious tat.

Our house was at the end of a terrace next door to a kindly, toothless old milkman called Bing and his family. Even from a young age, though, I sensed a real friction between us and the other families on the estate, most of whom I think perceived us as distant and aloof. The unruly boys next door would thump and cackle and play heavy metal until late into the evening, and there was a coterie of little thugs who would shout abuse at my dad and spend all day kicking footballs at the corrugated iron fence right outside our house, trampling on my mum's flowers and cruelly shattering her brittle, fictional Edwardian idyll. Indeed, our homemade Arts and Crafts-inspired world must have sat uncomfortably with the popular Zeitgeist of Status Quo T-shirts and plastic furniture. Our mother made most of our clothes so we must have looked very different from the corduroyed hordes, and would often be mocked and provoked. I don't think our dad's growing reputation as Haywards Heath's answer to Edith Sitwell or my mother's habit of sunbathing nude in the garden really helped, but slowly we were accepted and absorbed within the community, although we were always seen as outsiders – 'that lot with the piano in their kitchen'.

Outside each block of houses there were little grassy spaces where all the kids would compete in endless games of football. The estate would be ringing with the sounds of play, and tribes of little ruffians would bustle around on their Chopper bikes with their threats and their air pistols. Years later, whenever I returned, I was always struck by the absence of this; the grassy areas mute and childless now the generations had grown, the estate left to the greying parents – unwell, divorced and abandoned, like a line from 'North Country Blues'.

2

Everything we owned was either homemade or second-hand. My mother, my sister and I would be jumble sale regulars; battling the elbowing pensioners every Saturday afternoon at the local village hall. Ornaments, books, even underwear were snapped up for a few coppers and ferried home. Somehow I can still feel the second-hand purple nylon pants my mum used to make me wear. My mother ran our household on the proverbial shoe-string. She had been a child during post-war rationing so absolutely nothing was wasted or thrown away. She would pick wild nettles and mushrooms to make salad and soup, and pluck dead birds and skin rabbits to eat in stews. She would always be sewing; an arsenal of pins in her mouth, Cleopatra make-up and her hair done up like Elizabeth Taylor. Countless winter evenings while my dad was at work were spent sitting crouched around the fireplace listening to the quiet, gentle sound of needle on cloth as the firewood spat and crackled awaiting the dreaded scrape of my father's key twisting in the lock heralding the lottery of his mood. His meagre wage didn't allow much extravagance and my mother was always forced to buy cheap meat – chewy, fatty cuts and offal and veiny liver. Waste was forbidden, however, and we were not allowed to leave the table until we had finished every morsel on our plates. On those dreaded evenings when steak and kidney pudding was plonked in front of us, I was simply unable to comply, and would regularly sit alone for hours at the round, white, Formica kitchen table gagging and sobbing into my food until late in the evening when my furious mother eventually gave in and angrily threw my scraps away. The experience has left me with a lifelong hatred of meat, and must have left me hungry too, because Blandine and I began to hide and hoard food in our bedrooms.

Whenever there were snacks or spare scraps of things we actually liked, we would pocket them and ferry them secretly up to our bedrooms to be squirrelled away for times of hunger. I remember my mum used to make these savoury, twisty Marmite tarts, which I loved and would smuggle into my room to store under my bed in an old cardboard box that had once contained a pair of my dad's headphones. I became so obsessive about this little hoard that I started to forget the original point and ended up keeping it far too long. One day my mother confronted me angrily with my box full of mouldy, mildewy, rotting pastry after discovering it while cleaning, and I spent the rest of the day in a state of exposed, gloomy shame, never daring to repeat the cardinal sin of wasting food again. But looking back, she was a remarkable woman: incredibly creative and practical and stoical, and in her own way as hard as flint. Apart from a cheap electric oven we had no mod cons so she washed and dried all of our clothes by hand, something that seems unbelievable to my pampered twenty-first-century self. In her crusade to economise during the winter she would use the lukewarm contents of our hot water bottles to do the washing. There was no central heating in the house, just a small fireplace in the lounge and a little paraffin heater in the kitchen. The coal black mornings were brutal, and the ritual of lighting and maintaining the fire assumed a religious status. My mother was the high priestess, and we were her acolytes; fetching and carrying kindling and bits of old newspaper to hold over the flue to make the fire draw. On damp afternoons she would be crouched on the floor blowing at the smouldering embers, her hands smelling of woodsmoke and a line of worry etched across her forehead.

As well as holding the household together she used to make most of our clothes, and when she wasn't reading or painting or tending to the fire you could often find her kneeling on the mustard-coloured carpet with a pair of dress-maker's scissors in her hands, hunched over a sewing pattern – a sort of tailor's blueprint made out of gossamer thin paper that you would use to cut around fabric to assemble and stitch together parts of dresses and trousers and shirts. When my sister reached those self-conscious teenage years, she insisted that my mother sew in her own fake 'brand' label into one pair of cords so that she didn't feel too different to the other girls in their Levi's and Lee Coopers. The only time I remember being bought any clothes was when my mother forked out for a new winter coat for me when I was about eight. I wore it for the first time at a kid's party that was at a little boy's house out in the countryside on a small ramshackle farm. I got involved in a mud fight with all the other boys and turned up back home caked and splattered. My mother greeted me with an anger more wild than I ever remember, flying into a screaming, terrifying rage and setting about viciously slapping my bare legs. This was something that she would normally reserve for especially grave transgressions and was usually administered with a stern control, but this one time it assumed a sort of demented fury. I suppose the unforgiving, thankless, exhausting task of trying to keep a grip on the family's meagre purse strings had brought her to a kind of snapping point, and she simply couldn't contain herself as the frustrations finally spilled over.

Whereas my father's family was originally from Kentish Town, my mother was from Sussex country stock. Her own mother had died of breast cancer before I was born, and her father had moved and remarried, his loyalty so reapportioned to his new family that my sister and I only ever met him once; a prickly, uncomfortable afternoon hunched over tea-cups in a small house in Lewes when I was about eight. Mum used to trundle around the village on a sturdy, blue tricycle to the back of which my father had fixed a large wooden box. When it wasn't carrying groceries it would house her beloved Welsh springer spaniel, Misty, who would loll and pant and slobber as my mother pumped away at the pedals and the world looked on arch-eyebrowed and quizzical. In her more relaxed moments my mother was delicate and romantic, and would sit painting and listening to Joni Mitchell or The Stones on her little plastic portable cassette deck. As her single, solitary indulgence she would very occasionally allow herself the luxury of a can of Carnation condensed milk. It must have been some rare treat that she had been allowed during her bleak, austere childhood as it was the one thing that somehow seemed to make her vulnerable again; the frosty robes of control that she normally wore discarded as she sat there at the kitchen table smiling and purring like a little girl, spooning the white goo into her mouth. She was warm and loving and kind too, and I was obsessed with the possibility of her death.

Occasionally she would wear a wig, which she kept on a surreal-looking polystyrene head on her dressing table, and in a kind of sixties hangover she would back-comb and lacquer her hair, and would always be spraying herself with hairspray. I was convinced that inhaling too much of it would give her cancer, and like all sons was terrified of being denied her warmth and love. The twin fears which loomed on the landscape of my psyche like Isengard and Mordor around this time were this obsession about the malign effects of hairspray and the ever-present threat of nuclear attack which during the early eighties, when the world was still locked in the paranoid grip of the Cold War, seemed like a genuine possibility, and was regularly exacerbated and worried by the ever-irresponsible, ever-self-serving popular press. People were forever lugubriously poring over projected blast-damage maps or speculating gloomily about whether surviving or being immediately vaporised would be preferable in the gruesome event, and these kind of glum discussions meandered their way to our kitchen table where my mother would pontificate grimly about the agony of being burnt by melting nylon clothes, or about whether we would have time to save the rabbits. She was a voracious reader, and when she wasn't painting or sewing she would sit, stockinged feet up on the settee, lost in her novel while I clung to her, burying my head against her arm and plaguing her with interruptions about the plot and asking her if there were any pictures I could look at. Her love of literature must have bled through as even though it lay fairly dormant in me as a young man my appetite for books now borders on the rapacious.

Apart from the standard C. S. Lewis/Tolkien fantasy stuff the only serious novel that really dug into my consciousness as a boy was Orwell's *1984*. It's a book I regularly return to, enjoying how the intriguing process of re-reading it within a different period of my life can tease out new nuances of meaning. The well-documented presciences are, of course, fascinating but for me the real essence of the novel is its core love story. Quite early on I became aware that essentially the vast majority, if not all, art is in some way about love. Years later I began to apply this to my own writing, always framing songs within a human, emotional context, and allowing the dramas and frictions between people to be the vehicle that reveals further, wider truths. Any later interpretation of our music as being 'apolitical' has always struck me as over-literal; social comment surely not being just something that's limited to the primary colours of party politics.

A tiny literary seed must have been planted in me because in the late seventies I started to keep diaries. Completely forgotten about until now, they lived in a cardboard box for decades, following me mutely from house to house quietly waiting for their moment. Unfortunately, their moment is still to come as they failed to turn out to be the illuminating, revealing exposé of my early life that I'd hoped for when I came to write this. Sadly, they're just a dull litany of weather reports and trips to the shops, a drab timetable of school lessons and exam results lacking in any sort of insight or description, or anything interesting really. Even when events that now seem seismic happened, I seem to have blithely glossed over them, preferring to enthuse about what we had for dinner or the score of a football game. What a 'deeply boring young man' I must have been. Maybe Morrissey was right after all. I suppose I had yet to acquire any sort of emotional depth or any sense of perspective. Subjects like the complex landscape of my parents' marriage are represented by the odd sentence like *Mum and*

Dad had a row, revealing myself to be an unusually myopic and self-centred child. I think my mother especially kept me safely wrapped up in a warm, cosy blanket of delusion, never daring to betray her fears about the shifting, shaking fault-lines upon which our brittle world rested. It wasn't until I was well into adolescence that I remember having any sort of meaningful, honest conversation with her. She preferred to communicate through chats about books or TV programmes, or more often just through those tender, primal channels that mothers and sons often use.

Blandine, however, was much more perceptive. During the seventies and the early eighties my parents were still young, and as a concession to youth would throw parties at our house. It was always a magical and fascinating experience for Blandine and me who, exiled to upstairs, would hover by the banister listening to the bustle and chatter, the shrieks and the chink of glasses and breathe in the illicit, wafting fumes of alcohol and cigarette smoke as we perched high on the fringe of the adults' mysterious, exotic world. The next morning we would wake up early while my parents were still sleeping it off, tip-toe downstairs and step gingerly amongst the debris, making sense of the clues like detectives piecing together a mystery. I'll always remember finding a pair of discarded tights behind a curtain and wondering why Blandine found it so intriguing. Of course, my naive child's mind didn't understand the implications. Once the detective work was over, we would hurry about drinking the dregs that were sitting in the tumblers and glasses that still littered the tiny lounge and kitchen; downing the stale fingers of alcohol and thrilling to the intoxicating, sticky mixtures and the heady sense of transgression. I'm not sure how many would have belonged to my father, however, as he was almost a complete teeto-taller. I think his childhood dealing with the sharp end of my grandfather's alcoholism had coloured him hugely, and apart from the odd small glass of sherry at Christmas I don't think I ever saw him drink. Tea was his obsession, and it's one that I have inherited from him. He would forever be hovering by the steaming kettle, spooning loose leaves into the pot with a little, squat, tarnished silver spoon. After long nights at work he would lie in bed until late in the morning, and when he eventually woke up would bang savagely on the bedroom floor with a stick as a signal for my mum to bring him his tea, something that she would unhesitatingly do. Nowadays, rituals like that sound horribly misogynistic and primitive, but my parents had one of those old-fashioned, unwritten and probably unspoken agreements where the division of labour within the marriage was very clearly defined; my father earned the money and expected my mother to do pretty much everything else. I never once remember him cleaning or washing up, or, despite the fact that he had trained as a chef, ever helping with the cooking. Instead, he would sit at the table and brood, and insult my mother's food if the menu strayed in any way from the unadventurous 'meat and two veg'. Hilariously, he would even refer to spaghetti Bolognese as 'foreign muck', and when he'd finished pushing the food around his plate would slide it towards the centre of the table and make a sort of theatrical moue and a dismissive, fey, flapping gesture with his hands as a sign for my mother to take it away. The hierarchy of his household was for him very strictly defined; he was an Englishman and this was his castle, and as his marriage wore on he increasingly began to regard even his wife as chattel. This whole archaic equilibrium seemed to function for a while but, as my sister and then later I myself emerged from the numbing cocoon of childhood, we began to question his authority and clash with him in inevitable, endless, adolescent skirmishes.

I was a snotty, sniffy, slightly maudlin sort of boy raised on Salad Cream and milky tea and cheap meat, always scowling in photographs and a little bit downcast – not nihilistic or depressive really, but definitely glum, and always slightly befuddled. My mother once painted an unintentionally hilarious portrait of me, which I still own, depicting me standing gloomily in a field wearing a blue track suit with my hand poised over a packet of Sainsbury's salt and vinegar crisps, a sort of jowly, puffy, mournful expression on my face as I gaze disinterestedly into the middle distance. Crisps were one of the few foods I really craved as a child, and I clearly remember a fantasy I would occasionally allow to spool in my head whereby when I was grown up and had enough money I would buy myself a small mountain of them. It's something I really should do one day just to commune with my ten-year-old self. Like most young children I loved sweets, and when I was a little older would regularly take my 20p weekly pocket money up to an old-fashioned shop in the village called Harold's and buy a quarter pound of rainbow drops or cough candy: sticky twists of mentholated boiled sugar kept on shelves in big glass jars and scooped out and weighed and placed in plain little white paper bags. Harold himself was a sort of hulking, muttering gargoyle, always faintly irritated that any child would have the temerity to want to hand over their money to him, and the whole shop had an ancient, gloomy calm, like you had somehow just stumbled into the previous century. All that sugar rotted my teeth, of course, which meant that a seemingly large period of my childhood was spent being dragged to the dentist's in Haywards Heath. For a child of the seventies, the experience of visiting an NHS dentist before modernity had made the whole thing vaguely bearable was truly terrifying, and something I dreaded with a cold, penetrating, almost sickening fear. I would lie stiff and cowering with my mouth clamped open in one of those huge, wipe-clean, pale-green reclining chair things as the dentist jabbed and gouged and poked and drilled while I squeezed at my mother's hand and tried to make it through the tears and the horrible pain. After the ordeal I would usually stumble, bloody-mouthed and vomiting down Haywards Road to the house of the only member of my extended family that had a bit of money: my dad's Auntie Eva, my great-aunt, who lived by the park in a nice, old, red-brick Victorian house that smelled of string and spring flowers. On Saturday mornings, our family and a whole tribe of cousins would dutifully troop round to her house to have a coin or two pressed into our palms, and on the occasional evening we would crowd into her 'front room', sit on her plastic-protected furniture and gaze in marvel at her colour television. We only managed to afford a TV ourselves in the mid-seventies and even then it was just a tiny black and white set. She had married a fairly successful businessman, my uncle Jim, and then lost him to a stroke one fateful early spring, leaving her childless and with a kind of inherited status as the family matriarch. Her brother, my great-uncle Harry, was a kindly but mysterious chap with a bald shiny head and little tufts of hair growing above his ears which made him look a little like a koala bear, and who referred to 10p pieces as 'florins'. He had lodgings in Pimlico and worked at Claridge's as a handyman. He would often stay the weekend with his sister and regale us with tales of Eastern European princesses and city opulence.

He was a confirmed bachelor and there was never a mention of a girlfriend. He was probably gay but born into a generation where public acceptance was impossible. In later years, Auntie Eva started to suffer from dementia. Her observations about the neighbours' houses slowly moving towards her on stilts, or her habit of leaving a biscuit by my photo and then complaining to my dad that I hadn't eaten it seemed surreal and hilarious at first, but soon assumed a darker edge as the condition ground grimly on.

My dad's sister, my auntie Jean, was a spirited, rambunctious woman who was obsessed with cats and Elvis Presley, and would totter and clop in her high heels and miniskirt around Haywards Heath under a huge, swaying, dyed-blonde beehive hair-do. She was the manageress of the local branch of Dorothy Perkins and lived with her husband, a sweet, meek man called Vic, in a flat above the shop on South Road with their burgeoning brood of children, a white long-haired cat called Kinky and a large illuminated tank full of tropical angel fish. I remember she used to drink Babycham out of those small painted seventies' glasses, and my mum once made her a purple draught excluder in the shape of a snake. She is only a misty, washy memory for me, though, as her life ended in 1980 in a tragedy of almost iconic scale. She was found dead in a car with a man, who was presumed to be her lover, after they both succumbed to carbon monoxide fumes. As a child, overhearing the babble and conjecture at the time, it was unclear to me whether it was an accident or a suicide pact or even murder, as the gossip-mongers and the tittle-tattlers speculated and raked over the scant facts. I think the coroners returned an inconclusive verdict of 'misadventure', which only added fuel to the fires of rumour that burned fiercely in our sleepy town. It was naturally a drama of giant proportions within the family and a crushing tragedy to her surviving children and husband. It formed the inspiration for a song I wrote well over a decade later called 'She's Not Dead', where I tried to borrow some of the detail to paint a probably highly stylised sketch of the heartbreaking episode. One of the original lines was 'carbon monoxide sang as the engine ran', and to be honest I don't know why I didn't keep it. It seems strange to me now, and not a little callous, that I can sit here and talk about how I have turned personal events that have crushed and redirected people's lives into songs. Part of me feels that it's a somewhat shaming and trivial thing to do, and I hope I've never cheapened anyone's memory, but I think it's important to realise that art generally is just a process of documenting and interpreting and channelling one's experiences and turning them into something that lives in a place beyond reality. In my defence, at least the song is a good song, if that doesn't sound too glib, and the characters in it hopefully have a certain grace and dignity. Well, that was honestly the intention.

My mother loved to roam in the countryside and be amongst the trees and the twittering things, so fine weekends were usually spent wandering on the South Downs. Sometimes she and my sister would embark on epic three-day journeys across the downland. When my dad and I went along they were relatively painless but would usually double as a foraging expedition – blackberries in the late summer and mushrooms in the autumn. If we weren't tramping around the Wealdland pathways you could find us visiting castles or churches. My dad became obsessed with brass rubbing, and we regularly had to stand around draughty rural naves while he kneeled, frowning over his waxen effigies, telling us about their distant, irrelevant lives. We would often have to endure onerous journeys to faraway transepts and stand around for hours, bored and distracted. Our holidays were spent almost exclusively in Britain (I first flew at the age of thirteen), usually in hired camper-vans or in stationary caravan parks in places like Devon or Suffolk over depressing rainy October half-terms. The caravans were even more claustrophobic than our tiny house and always smelled of wet cardboard and Harpic. It rained and it rained, and we spent endless resentful hours cooped up listening to the radio, my father crouched, sulking over his guide books and my mother fussing around making cups of tea in the tiny kitchenettes.

Back home, our lives trundled along. Behind the rubbish tip the local kids had discovered an earlier, presumably pre-war section of the dump and the craze of 'bottle-digging' was born. We would traipse over the wasteland armed with trowels and spades, and come back laden with antique pots and jars and dark-coloured glass-ware emblazoned and embossed with archaic-looking and obsolete brand-names: bloater paste pots, 'codswallop' bottles containing little glass marbles and even small phials darkly warning of 'poison' in raised glass letters. The cream of these would be ferried off to the local antique shops and sold for a few pence, only to be glimpsed again a week or so later, sparkling and clean and horribly marked up.

The woods and wilderness behind the estate became a kind of lawless playground for all of us kids. Once you stepped beyond the order of the concrete and on to Wealdland clay you entered an unruly empire of teenage tribes, a kind of *Lord of the Flies* disorder with air-pistolled gangs and minor violence; a self-regulating world that the local adults rarely bothered to enter. There would be little coteries of kids who would build camps – basically a small area where someone had dragged an old mattress and some other bits of household rubbish to give a vaguely domesticated feel – in which we would sit around and drink lemonade from family-sized bottles and play cards and gossip about football. Inevitably, your camp would be wrecked if a rival gang discovered it: the mattress pissed on and the 'furniture' smashed. One year the older boys built an elaborate underground warren complete with 'bedrooms' and corrugated iron roofs and candle-lit walls. It survived for a whole summer and was the back-drop to many rumorous episodes until it too eventually succumbed to vandalism and rainwater.

The first school I remember was one of those red-brick Victorian village primary schools, the kind that still have separate *Boys* and *Girls* entrances – the legacy of some skilled nineteenth-century stone-mason. It was a sweet and relatively happy time: a summery, hazy watercolour of tarmac playgrounds, conkers and five-a-side football, all bathed with that seemingly immutable, timeless, school smell of crayon-tips and sour milk and polished floors. It was troubled only by the pinched, irritated spectre of one Miss Holden, an old-fashioned, slightly terrifying teacher who approached the art of winnowing children a little like Miss Jean Brodie in the Muriel Spark novel. She would establish elites within her class and encourage them and goad them and expect excellence, and sometimes even folk dancing. I'm pleased to report that there is almost certainly no surviving photographic evidence of me with bells tied around my legs holding a Morris stave. These were the days before obsessive parental involvement in schools, when once the child was delivered into the classroom and the clock struck nine the teacher's rule became hegemonic. It was an absolutism that often bordered on abusive. I remember one poor child, who had become somewhat a target, being dragged down the corridor by his hair like in a scene from *The Wall* while being screamed at for being like 'the cow's tail – always behind!'. But despite a few pockets of unpleasantness, I can't pretend that my time there wasn't relatively carefree.

The murkier years were yet to come when I was dumped unceremoniously into the large local comprehensive, Oathall: a forbidding, bleak nineteen thirties building that serviced the wider surrounding area. It seemed enormous and daunting to my guileless eleven-year-old self, and indeed the sheer volume of shrieking, grey-trousered urchins was intimidating. There were about thirty-five children per class and nine classes in every year, so the school was home to about fifteen hundred kids. It was huge, it was loud, and at times it could be terrifying. I arrived there in the late seventies when tribalistic pop culture was arguably at its peak and the playgrounds were awash with rival gangs. Even the younger kids would try to adapt themselves to the gestures of their various adopted groups: the punks spiking up their hair, the headbangers growing theirs, the mods in their Parkas and differently tied ties, and the Rude boys with shorn hair and a carpet of Two Tone badges across their regulation, maroon school jumpers. All of the tribes were relatively harmless except the skinheads, who flirted in an ill-informed way with hard right politics and adopted the style and belligerence of those early eighties racist thug groups like the National Front and the British Movement. As I'd formed early close friendships with one boy whose family were from Nigeria and another whose were Indian, I was closer to the constant threat of harm, and got to witness their disgusting, spittle-flecked spite close up: their sixteen-hole boots, their sticks and their hateful, hateful words. The school was awash with the kind of minor violence and intimidation that the teachers were unable or unwilling to do anything about. The time-honoured patterns of persecution – of the weak by the strong, of the unworldly by the knowing – found a sort of strangely comfortable acceptance within its concrete playgrounds and chain-link fences. It was only because I was fairly tall and good at sport that I escaped the ever-present threat of 'the bog-wash' or worse – the regular, vicious, gang beatings that groups of unruly older kids would dish out to those younger boys they thought wouldn't fight back.

I never bought bondage trousers or dyed my hair but fell in love with punk rock music quite early on. My father's classical obsession seemed somehow provoking and confrontational and non-inclusive, and led me to embrace punk's starkness and primitive, vital energy with the added sense that instead of being part of an irrelevant, faded, bygone age, this was an expression of my life and the world I saw around me: the white dog shit on the pavements, the vandalised, piss-stained phone boxes and the constant miasma of threat and fear and that somehow, through its expression of truth, it contained its own equally valuable nobility. *Never Mind The Bollocks* was, I'm still proud to say, the first album I ever bought and it heralded a lifelong love affair with alternative music. I scraped the money together doing odd jobs and paper rounds, and marched down to Haywards Heath market one Sunday to buy it, scurrying back home with my prize where it sat semi-permanently on the turntable of my record player for months like some sort of undefeated champion. Of course, living in the outer suburbs you acquired trends and fashions literally years after they had been and gone in London, so the Pistols' career arc, like the light from a distant star, had already passed by the time I bought the record. Nevertheless, it seemed utterly, utterly vital and I fell into its grooves, learning every moment of its beautiful insurrection. Still today, I often use 'Bodies' as intro music, its carnal, primitive scream never failing to create the same Pavlovian response it created in me all those years ago sitting there in my little bedroom staring out over Newton Road. From there I started listening to what was more contemporary stuff – the post-punk early eighties netherworld of bands like Crass and Discharge – music that politicised punk's restless disorder. I would be upstairs in my room playing *The Feeding Of The 5,000* as loud as my cheap sound system would allow while downstairs my dad would be blasting out the *Enigma Variations*. If you stood somewhere on the stairs you would be able to experience a bizarre Eno-esque hybrid. Crass fascinated me. Gee Vaucher's nightmarish, surreal and highly politicised sleeves were somehow both beautiful and intimidating; timelessly elegant but acerbic, relevant and taut with threat. The songs dealt with the kind of themes I'd previously thought alien to pop: warfare, domestic abuse, religion, indoctrination, and everywhere a restless, questioning, dissenting voice dissecting and criticising social mores and accepted political structures. I always played the albums at 33 rpm, not realising they were intended to be played at 45, and I fell in love with the slowed down, hellish yowl that seemed so in keeping with the content. One day, though, someone told me of my mistake and when I heard the music for the first time at the intended speed somehow the magic was lost.

My paper round was pretty much my only source of income and so became essential in order that I could buy records. I would haul myself out of bed at five-thirty some mornings, and blindly stagger and wobble around the sleepy cul-de-sacs of Haywards Heath on my bike pushing copies of the *Mid-Sussex Times* through aluminium letterboxes. For this I was paid £3.25 a week – slave labour by today's standards but a princely sum in 1981. With an extra £1.25 from my Sunday paper round, I had enough to feed myself with a steady drip of vinyl: *Brand New Age*, *The Stations Of The Crass*, *Sid Sings* and many other such hallowed minor gems found their way back to my bedroom and on to the altar of my turntable. It was an old, third-hand Boots Audio thing that my sister had given me when she left home. The potentiometers were ancient so one of the speakers would often splutter and crackle like it was clearing its throat, and the sound was scratchy and utterly lacking any real body or heft. But I've always wondered if its lack of precision and clarity didn't somehow inform the way I began to listen to music. Because the stereo was so thin-sounding I guess I learned to not listen to the bottom end in music, and I didn't really get the point of the bass guitar until I was well into my twenties. For me it was all about the top-line and the song, and in the same sort of way that Pete Townshend wrote versions of pop hits that he'd apparently misheard, so I began to hear music through the distorting prism of my broken hi-fi and sieve out the bits that didn't seem important. I became oblivious to any subtlety in music, and fell in love with songs that spoke to me clearly and simply, just following the power of the chord sequences and the words and the melodies. This eventually fed into how I started to write – forever stumbling around searching for the big, billowing chorus and the coup de grâce of the simple, killer hook. Anyway, it's always, always been about making things your own; imitation will only get you so far. The parameters of my ability, though at first a limitation, actually ended up being a strength as I incrementally developed the only style I could – my own.

As music became increasingly important I started to make friends with kids who shared my love. Some had a bizarre habit of switching tribes literally overnight. My friend Simon Stevenson, a bright funny boy with a huge mane of curly Marc Bolan hair, with whom I'm still close, did this one day, arriving at school in cowboy boots and a studded denim jacket. He'd jumped ship and become a headbanger. He sold me his punk 45s and introduced me to that exciting narrow band of punk/metal cross-over music like Sabbath's *Paranoid* and *Motörhead* by Motörhead, records drenched in snake-bite and patchouli and the throb of teenage danger. Simon Stevenson is the first of four Simons you will meet in these pages. For some probably generational reason it's a name that's followed me through my life, and is attached to four very different but very important characters.

Another local boy I met, this time a John, lived

up the road in a similarly depressing red-brick doll's house. We would scurry off to his bedroom and play his punk singles, things like UK Decay and Sham 69 and The Cockney Rejects. We would learn all the words and imitate the postures and think we were both terribly grown-up. One day we were playing some dreadful plastic-punk offering, and his mum, Betty – a sweet, kind woman with curly, white, bottle-blonde hair – burst into the room, outraged at the swearing and tore the record off the turntable and smashed it in a kind of *Daily Mail* rage. The sense of transgression was exquisite and our fascination was piqued.

Whether it was partly some sort of reaction to this general whiff of rebellion or not, the same boy and I once got into deep water at school for compiling a list of bizarre and hilarious imaginary punishments for all the teachers. It was a grotesque litany of almost medieval retribution including things like having them 'hung by their hair from a helicopter' etc. etc. The details were gory and exquisite, and were intended to have the same sort of macabre but darkly comic tone as the Edward Lear illustrations of which I had become so fond. Snatched by the hands of authority one lunch-time, however, they were soon stripped of any humour and interpreted as deeply pernicious, and we were forced to undergo the subtle but humiliating public ordeal of standing, heads hung in shame, in the busy central thoroughfare of the school known as Piccadilly Circus as the masses swarmed by and sniggered knowingly. I think the most effective punishment though was having the inner, dark machinations of one's febrile imagination, no matter how comically intended, made so public, and for years I squirmed, wondering if the document had survived embarrassingly 'on my record'. It planted a powerful seed in me as I realised how darkly seductive, but also how treacherous and dangerous, words can be.

When I was a young child I don't think I was particularly conscious of us being poor. I was too locked within my selfish, narrow child's world to really have any sense of perspective. It never occurred to me that other children didn't help their mothers pluck dead birds or skin rabbits, or that most people didn't just huddle around a single open fire in the winter evenings for warmth; not that Oathall was full of rich kids – it was a Haywards Heath comprehensive school – but I gradually became aware that our lives, if not unique, were certainly marginal. One particular grim ritual forced home the cold, hard truth. As my father earned so little I was entitled to free school meals. For some reason, rather than doing it privately and discreetly, the unfortunate kids that fell into this unenvied little band were forced by the school to queue up in public for their special tickets in the large echoing canteen in full view of all the other sniggering, jeering children. To say it was a humiliating experience is a crushing understatement. It was like a Dickensian workhouse scene; a punishment for being poor, like being pilloried or put in the stocks: brutal, completely unnecessary and pointlessly cruel. The experience was truly scarring and made me utterly fearful of poverty. The memory of it often haunts me and makes me shudder with the fear that my own boys would ever have to go through anything nearly so horrible. A similarly crushing experience happened when on a Christmas day trip to London my father's car broke down right outside Harrod's department store in Knightsbridge. My mother, my sister and I had to get out and push while my father twisted frantically at the ignition key and pumped at the pedals to a dissonant chorus of angry car horns. The symbolism seems ridiculously appropriate and almost grotesque, our poverty spotlit against a backdrop of opulence and power; four insignificant figures lost in a desperate struggle while symbols of wealth gazed indifferently on.

3

Living with my father's eccentricity there was always a sense that his mood could suddenly, capriciously sour and that the house would be plunged into a strange, dark theatre of Pinteresque tension. Paranoid episodes would overcome him and he would often complain that people were watching or talking about him. Towards the end of his life, when loneliness and depression had won its grim struggle, he lived in almost complete darkness, the curtains closed, convinced that someone outside was always observing him. Looming like a shadow on the edge of Haywards Heath was

St Francis Hospital, a forbidding red-brick asylum built in the 1850s, home to the mentally unstable and source of much black humour and local legend and provenance of threat and rumour. In his darker, more reflective moments he was haunted by its spectre, terrified of 'ending up' within its dank Victorian passageways, lost to a netherworld of gurneys and burly, indifferent carers.

He was born into a family that not so much didn't value education as didn't really seem to be aware of it. You were born within your class and didn't aspire beyond it. I suppose the culture of the working-class 'boy done good' had yet to reach its footballing, pop-singing, nineteen sixties zenith, so my father, despite being an intelligent and sensitive boy, was marched unencouraged through the strata of low-level education, eventually finding himself channelled into a catering college in Brighton from which he drifted into a series of dead-end menial jobs that never offered him much satisfaction or his family much security. For a short while he was an ice-cream man, a gardener and a window cleaner, and during a period in the late seventies he bizarrely became a swimming-pool attendant at the local leisure centre despite the fact that he couldn't swim. Heaven knows how he qualified for the post. I dreaded Tuesdays, which was the day of my class's visit there for swimming lessons, knowing I would be mercilessly tormented by the other kids pointing at him and collapsing in fits of sniggering. When in the eighties he eventually settled on a modest career as a taxi driver his unreliable car became a symbol of our insecurity. By this time he'd upgraded from the Morris Traveller to a third-hand, mid-range Volvo which was forever breaking down and over-heating. My mother, my sister and I would wait anxiously for news of its well-being like fretful parents with a sickly child, painfully aware of how the outcome influenced our vicissitudes. Looking back, I suppose these pressures took their toll. Although he was never materialistic or ambitious, this constant cloud of anxiety and financial stress must have been responsible for the fissures and cracks that began to appear in him. The angry clashes with my mother would storm and spark while my sister and I would cower in our bedrooms, locked in a horrible, compulsive trance, unable to listen yet unable not to; sheltering from the accusations and the vitriol as the thudding, angry words and choruses of crashing crockery and slamming doors made their way up through the paper-thin walls. I know myself how supporting a family can feel like an overwhelming task sometimes, so my father's struggles on what was effectively a bread-line wage take on a selfless, noble aspect that at the time I was completely unaware of, submerged as I was within my child's world of football kits and double maths.

As well as an imperious, dusty historicism, my dad had a genuinely bawdy streak. He could tell filthy, ribald jokes and would forever be making embarrassing comments, often in public which could feel mocking and often cruel. At the softer end of the scale there would be suggestive, priapic Steptoe-isms about 'not looking at the mantelpiece when you're stoking the fire' and so on, but the business end could be graphic and tawdry and lubricious, and often wince-inducing. This got more uncomfortable as I became older and drifted into prickly adolescence, but I remember it happening from a very young age, so he evidently didn't bother to employ any sort of filter for the children. Perhaps it was a legacy of years rubbing shoulders with fellow unskilled workers in dead-end jobs where he had picked up the colourful language of the playgrounds and of the canteens and the kitchens as a means to fit in and assimilate, and probably to defend himself as he was physically slight. My grandfather's violent, drunken rages had left him with a creed of physical pacifism – a noble attempt to break that ugly chain of inheritance for which I am forever grateful – but words had armed him with a different kind of weaponry that he would often use mercilessly. His shameless, sometimes vicious, turns of phrase must have informed the tone of many of my early songs, which I was often conscious of wanting to make similarly lewd, littering them with swear words and sexual imagery, enjoying the genuine shocking power that the language of the street can wield; a kind of Gilbert and George-esque world of toilet graffiti and felt-tip-scrawled cubicles. You can hear it in the verses of 'My Insatiable One', 'To The Birds' and 'She's Not Dead', and in the dark suggestion of something like 'Pantomime Horse'. It was probably partly a desire on my part to be confrontational but there was also an element of my wanting to use real language, not some sanitised series of anodyne pleas-antries, and I suppose that was inherited from my father's occasional rough estuary-isms.

His lack of a formal education led him to seek out the knowledge that he felt he'd been denied. He became obsessed with history and would probe us with endless quizzes about the battle of this or the fall of that. We were forever being harried and hustled around castles and churches and stately homes, sitting in countless soggy National Trust car parks drinking stewed tea from Thermos flasks as the rain pounded angrily on the car roof. Having been born within the fading influence of the British Empire, he was a committed royalist and could recite the order of succession and dates of birth and death of every monarch since William the Conqueror, and would regularly stand to attention and salute the national anthem during BBC2's Closedown. We started collecting the symbols of this autocracy – old British coins and stamps – and would trawl through junk shops and tatty antique fairs searching for the elusive bargain that would turn our fortunes. Looking back, this was a golden age when I was still essentially a sweet, simple little boy unfettered by the fractious seeds of adolescence, and who still believed the myth in which all young sons need to believe: that my dad was strong and faultless and always right. There was a point when we were inseparable, lost and locked together as we rummaged through our dusty world of Penny Blacks and First Day Covers; when I was still too young to challenge him in any way, and he was still romantic enough about parenthood to want to try to give me the kind of loving bond with my dad that he had never had with his. Perhaps he was living through me the upbringing denied him by my grandfather's angry fists and, indeed, whenever I was bought the ubiquitous seventies Airfix model kits, it was always my dad who insisted on making them, exiling me to the role of spectator and denying me my imperfect child's touch. It was something that never felt excluding, though, merely considered and strangely caring. There was a sense that through kindness to me he was passing on kindness to a childhood spectre of himself. I have the same odd sort of feeling sometimes with my own boy as I gaze upon his vulnerable little form. It's probably one of the reasons nature makes sons look like their dads.

He started collecting military memorabilia, his centrepiece being a Napoleonic naval sword that he hung proudly above our little grey-tiled fireplace. The contrast between the grandeur of the antique and the scale of the room must have looked ridiculous, but it was something that he was proud to own, and he was forever polishing it and speculating about in which particular battle it might have seen action. Years later, during one of my ill-advised impromptu teenage parties thrown while my parents were out for the evening, a couple of gatecrashers stole it and were chased down the road and rugby-tackled by my good friend Simon Cambers who, thank god, had the wherewithal to react.

My dad also started picking up old coronation mugs, which began decorating the kitchen; his pride and joy being one depicting Edward VIII, the king who abdicated – probably some sort of rarity. It got smashed during one of my mother's rages, though, and I still own the badly glued, imperfect relic and all his other commemorative cups. When he died, Blandine and I were faced with the Herculean, heartbreaking task of sorting through all his stuff, and they were amongst the few trinkets I really wanted to keep; their quirky mix of the imperious and the mundane somehow capturing an essential thread of his character.

He loved eccentric, oddball Victoriana as well, and

when he wasn't listening to Liszt would read Edward Lear's strange and wonderful nonsense poems out loud to us, chewing deliciously over each mad stanza of 'The Jumblies' or 'The Dong with a Luminous Nose'. I may have acquired my love for internal rhyme from those dusty couplets, and became fascinated by their surreal, often macabre, accompanying illustrations of giant insects or people cutting their own fingers off. Today I often read exactly the same insane little verses to my own son, enjoying the sensation of mirroring the past and of a pleasing sense of continuity, a consciousness of being part of something bigger than oneself.

My father was always dressed immaculately, often in the three-piece suits that my mum had made for him. In the whole thirty-eight years that I knew him I never remember him once without a tie. In the black and white Box Brownie photos I have of him as a young man he's dressed in smart Rat Pack-style suits, his hair coiffed like James Dean, but the more louche styles of the seventies transformed him into a kind of crumpled Victorian dad with a hint of the Romanovs about him: bearded, elegant, reposed in a tatty, red, padded antique-silk dressing gown, and with a briar pipe permanently clamped between his tobacco-stained teeth spewing out plumes of smoke and turning the air thick and bluish. In a bizarre homage to another of his heroes, T. E. Lawrence, he somehow acquired full Arab robes and would often parade around his council house dressed like Peter O'Toole's double cast adrift in some bitterly ironic parallel universe.

In the early eighties my sister left home, bound for art college in Worthing, a faded, South Coast retirement resort dominated by the superannuated which became faintly mythical for me. I revelled in the off-kilter juxtaposition of the armies of shuffling pensioners and the restless, rowdy subculture of young art students. There, she met Tim, a young man who for a while became a bit like my older brother. He was a huge fan of sixties bands and his enthusiasm was contagious. Together they introduced me to all of that forgotten music – The Beatles, The Kinks, Bowie, The Who and Zeppelin – and all the pre-punk records that during the early eighties had been cast aside by fashion's relentless march. You have to remember that this was before glossy music monthlies or YouTube or shuffle culture or any real revisionism – when there was no expectation that anyone should bother to investigate the music of the past, and because of that they tended not to. Uncovering these things involved a kind of breathless, archaeological thrill. While other school kids were getting into Thompson Twins' chart pop or post-punk, I was starting to unearth records by Jefferson Airplane, Robert Wyatt and early Floyd, song-based relics from a hazy past. Vaguely echoing my father I revelled in the slight outsiderdom of this, enjoying being out of step and slightly perverse.

It was around this time that Blandine brought home a battered old Spanish guitar and a simple beginners' chord book. She taught me a few things and I fumbled around the fretboard, gamely attempting to master a few basic chord shapes. It must have sounded bloody awful as I thrashed away crudely around A, D and E, not realising for starters that you simply don't play a classical guitar like an acoustic, but it planted a seed and I soldiered on with a cloth-eared enthusiasm. I wrote a few simplistic ditties that aped the singer-songwriter genre and found that I could just about hold a note, so I started to enjoy toying with the interplay between words and melody, and began the first faltering steps on the path that would lead to a lifelong fascination with that elusive alchemy. It dawned on me that songs, like rabbit hutches or three-piece suits, could be things within reach that I might one day be able to make. I saw how their basic frameworks were constructed and that even though mine were as yet poorly assembled, crude and inelegant, they still somehow functioned no matter how primitively. From a very early age I remember being acutely conscious of melody in music. I have a vivid memory of lying on my parents' bed one afternoon while my mother fiddled around with her hair, humming to myself with my face pressed against the fusty white covers and thinking about the series of notes I was singing and how they worked against each other. It sounds obvious now, but I became aware that this was essentially how all music began – with someone playing around with notes – and that realisation somehow made music's creation less of a mystery. As almost everything at home was homemade the idea of making one's own songs didn't really seem like a stretch.

Looking back I can see how the melodies I wrote that ended up defining me were a strange but direct combination of things I was hearing at home. The bombast of my father's music was inescapable, and even though I would often balk at its pomposity I can't deny that I was subconsciously always trying to capture something of its drama. The storming intellectual arguments and sour, clashing debates we used to have about music had laid a foundation and made me highly opinionated on the subject, instilling in me a similar religious fervour and a view that, to adapt the old Bill Shankly adage: it wasn't just a matter of life and death – it was much more important than that. And it's an attitude I've never felt I should apologise for, despite how po-faced the haters might think it makes me look. Years later we were described by the press as 'the most humourless band since Joy Division' which was meant as a wry slight, but I only took it as a massive compliment; why shouldn't something as transforming and life-affirming and celestial as music have a heft and a gravity that transcends the trivial and the everyday? I've always really hated irony in music seeing it as a kind of cowardice, a mask to hide behind for those who don't have the bravery or conviction to really expose themselves. I have my father's wild-eyed passion to thank for the fact that I'm sometimes guilty of taking it very seriously and for the fact that during lengthy episodes of my life music has meant absolutely everything to me.

Bizarrely, it was my least favourite subject at school. I found it elitist and unengaging; a joyless exercise in reciting dates and learning mnemonics; a dusty, irrelevant litany of dry theories taught by a corduroy-suited fossil. Unbelievably, the same teacher had been at the school when my father was there a generation earlier and he had similarly failed to ignite any flame in him, at least in any formal sense. Instead, I turned to the other school kids and, like countless other suburban boys in countless other suburban towns, formed the inevitable first band. Mine was hilariously called Suave and Elegant. Beyond it possibly being some sort of silly wry comment on coiffured eighties pop, I have no idea why it was called that other than the fact that it amused us. 'Us' being myself cast as singer, Simon Stevenson on bass guitar and my impish, mischievous friend Simon Cambers, a fantastic drummer and all-round musician whose restless, manic spirit still never fails to make me smile. Simon and Simon had previously been in another school band called The Pigs, and they had a kind of band theme song called 'We Are The Pigs'. Years later, I would blithely steal the title but outrageously never credit them. I loved the brutal, homophonic meaning and wrote a lyric around it about a stylised riot – a kind of dark insurrection peppered with the suggestion of threat. By that point I had become obsessed with zoomorphism and felt I had made the title enough of my own for the steal to seem justified. In fact, mulling it over now, the idea of a band theme song is something I had thought original to my lyric for 'Trash', but I'm sure even that had some sort of primitive provenance with the original 'Pigs' and I'm sure there are probably other examples that predate both songs.

But I digress. Back to 1984, and by this point I'd taken to swanning around in a cheap lemon-yellow suit I'd picked up in a sale at Top Man. I imagine I thought it suggested a kind of Bowie-esque sophistication, but the truth was I probably looked more like a cut-price Cliff Richard. The two Simons were both into heavy rock and would listen to a whole gamut of bands that left me cold, like UFO and Rush, so I think there was probably a naive attempt by us to emulate that kind of overly complex, dull musicianship. We all loved the Pistols, though, and Bowie, but perversely, along with the classic seventies canon, we loved his earlier, vaudeville incarnation: the theatrical whimsy of songs like 'Please Mr. Gravedigger' and 'Karma Man' and 'Maid Of Bond Street'. The Simons also introduced me to Tyrannosaurus Rex, T. Rex's earlier folky prototype. We thought the often deliberately verbose, wryly mystic titles and odd, charming, hippyish songs were wonderful, and would sit there in my room gazing at the album sleeves, which seemed like a portal to a different age. The sleeves discarded and the cheap guitars back in our laps, we would sit ploughing through one or other of our two awful, tuneless songs cramped together in my tiny bedroom, and suddenly my dad would push the door open and march in braying and booing and laughing at us, a strange look on his face as his emotions flickered between amusement and pity. He could be extremely quixotic, a borderline fantasist even. Throughout my childhood he would hubristically bang on about how I was going to be a concert pianist, but never bothered to even think about getting me piano lessons or any sort of formal training. One day, though, he dragged a broken, old, upright piano home, but it sounded so awful that it just sat sulking in a corner of our kitchen for years, unused, untuned and unloved, taking up space and supporting tea-cups. Maybe it was part of that whole inevitable challenge between generations that pop music used to be so effective at instigating, but my picking up a guitar seemed to trigger a latent sense of betrayal in my father. Even when I was releasing successful records in the nineties I remember him muttering a waspish aside about how my 'little tunes' couldn't match up to the quality of Hector Berlioz or something similarly wounding. The only time I think I really impressed him with my career was when we eventually played the Royal Albert Hall and I sat him in a box to watch the performance. I think at last he could relate my work to the classical world with which he was so familiar, but even then after the gig he couldn't resist commenting that he thought the guitars were 'too distorted'. 'Well, Dad,' I said, 'they're supposed to be.'

I don't mean to come across as unkind in sharing these little memories of my father as I know some of them don't show him in the best light, but what I'm learning while writing this is that, as I uncover things about him that are buried deep in my memory, I'm also uncovering things about myself and the kind of person that I'm likely to become if left unchecked, so in that sense it's very important for me to be truthful. Understanding my dad is, of course, a way of understanding myself. Whenever anyone asks me today about the nature of my relationship with my father the most accurate adjective I can find is 'complicated'. He was a collection of fascinating people, some of which were charming and warm and kind and funny and loving, and some of which were belligerent and controlling and sardonic and cruel. One moment he would do sweet, selfless things like track me down on my paper round to bring me my coat because he was worried about me getting wet, and the next he would be distant and prickly and paranoid, and storm around accusing his family of 'ganging up on him'. His was a combative, challenging sort of love, but along with the challenge came a depth of empathy that was somehow special to my relationship with him. Every son has at some time gazed into the mirror and seen their father staring back at them, and if they haven't yet then they will do soon, because as you get older you find those familiar patterns and foibles you thought so unique to them repeating themselves in you. I assume a psychoanalyst would tell me that the frustrations I felt in him were frustrations and fears that I felt for myself that I projected on to him or something, but without wanting to drag this whole discussion towards that sort of dry, clinical lexicon it's important for me to acknowledge that my documentation and description of my dad *is* partly one of myself: a dissection of inheritance, an analysis of the links in the chain that bond father to son and beyond. Decades later, I wrote some lyrics about this whole thing in a song called 'I Don't Know How To Reach You' that tried to sketch a spectrum where I was just a point on a path between my dad and my own son. It's an idea that quietly obsesses me as the landscape of parenthood slowly reveals itself.

Anyway, my dad certainly never took my interest in pop music that seriously, and looking at my laughable lack of ability in those early years I would have to sympathise with him. Indeed, the idea of one of my boys following in my footsteps gives me night thoughts, and to advise them on embarking on such a precarious path would be ridiculous, I'm sad to say; the lonely dogged determination required, the blinkered arrogance, the long odds and the sheer luck involved in success seem almost insurmountable, and in the modern digital age the rewards incommensurate.

Even though I'm glad that they did, I don't really understand how my parents ever allowed me to pursue music as a career given that I had no training or particular early aptitude, so in many ways my dad's lack of encouragement was totally understandable.

My mother, however, was always less acerbic than my father; she would sit and hum our horrible tunes in a faithful spirit of cosy motherly support. She didn't see music as this angry battleground of charged opinion that my dad did, and her tastes were much more populist – mainly sixties folk that she would listen to while painting or sewing. She was always making something, creating something or mending something. This wonderful sense of purpose must have bled into me a little: the idea that if you wanted something you made it yourself. Slowly I started to apply that spirit to my clumsy fumblings with song-writing.

My father was outrageously outspoken about music, however, and would cruelly mock and poke at anything that wandered outside his narrow boundaries of taste. Once in much later years we again visited the Albert Hall to see a performance of Rachmaninoff's *Rhapsody on a Theme of Paganini*. Before the main event there was an experimental piece by Béla Bartók.

My dad hated it and as the last chords faded, in that split second between the final note and the first joyous rush of applause, he jumped to his feet and roared *'Rubbish!'* at the top of his voice, clear and loud against the stark, momentary silence. Five thousand shocked, angry faces swivelled towards us as I sat there throbbing with disbelief, my dad's face a strange mask of triumph and defiance.

4

The time came to sit some exams and I did okay, sleep-walking into A-level courses at Haywards Heath Sixth Form College – a blank, generic, institutional building just up from the railway station and cast adrift amongst a small sea of offices and lower-middle-class houses. At Oathall, if you were a bright kid you were automatically ushered towards the sciences and maths, presumably destined for some sort of dull, functional engineering-based career. The logic must have been that people from a comprehensive school in Haywards Heath simply didn't become artists or musicians. I always found physics absolutely fascinating, however, especially Newtonian mechanics, which seemed so neat and elegant and satisfying. It helped that our teacher, a Mr Bamford, was truly inspirational, one of those fabled, script-written educational alchemists who could fill with urgency and life what in others might come across as dry and dusty. Legend has it that after leaving teaching he unexpectedly became a priest, which only further added to his mystique and charisma. A-levels didn't similarly inspire me, though, and I found myself becoming bored with education and regretting my choices. To fill the void, music's magic and allure began to grip me, and I discovered a whole swathe of early eighties left-field records. Bands like The Cult, Joy Division, The Cocteau Twins, Lloyd Cole and most importantly The Smiths became regulars on my turntable, relegating UK Subs and Stiff Little Fingers to the dusty forgotten corners of my collection, where they languished, exiled and deposed like medieval kings.

I started hanging out with yet another Simon, this one a Holdbrook – a warm, thoughtful, sometimes troubled boy who shared my fascination with the murkier corners of life and with whom I felt the thrill of mutual outsiderdom; two small-town dreamers trapped in a dreary suburban cell, yearning for the thrill and promise beyond. Like a thousand other dreamers in a thousand other suburban towns we were convinced that our experience was unique, but it made it no less special that it wasn't. His family had a bit more money than mine so he lived in a more well-to-do part of town, but still nothing you'd call posh; the boxy houses were just a little less boxy, and they could afford to actually buy things rather than make them or find them, which to be honest probably seemed posh to me. As a form of escapism we tumbled into an idealised nineteen sixties chimera. It seemed like an antidote to the functional, grey concrete world we were born into, and in a way it helped me to assimilate the absence of my sister. She was always a strong, determined, fiercely independent person, and had left home years before leaving behind her empty north-facing bedroom, her record player and a stack of anachronistic vinyl. I would wander into her room and wistfully play her records, latching on to this music from the past because it seemed somehow a part of her. Like any younger sibling I looked up to her and probably massively romanticised her life at art college and, yes, I missed her terribly.

Simon and I would sit in his bedroom thrumming ineptly along on our cheap electric guitars and would write songs with unintentionally hilarious titles like 'String The Years Together Like Beads' or 'Homage To The Beatles'. It sounds highly comical now, but I think at the time it felt exciting and fresh and vaguely outré because it sat so uncomfortably with the popular Zeitgeist of Bryan Adams and Bruce Springsteen. Inspired by the romance of sixties psychedelia and through a fascination with Aldous Huxley's famous book we discovered the wonders of lysergic mushrooms: free, extremely potent and growing plentifully in the misty autumn fields that bordered the hinterlands of our humdrum town. On September mornings we would set our alarms and meet up, dazed and still sleep-fuddled, and traipse in Wellingtons and cagoules over the dewy autumn grass searching for the precious white cargo, which we would smuggle back home and brew into tea. The hours would merge and shift as we wandered dazed and aimless through the back streets and over the ring roads and roundabouts, marvelling at the perversity and lost in the labyrinths of our babbling thought. Years later I would write a song called 'Where The

Pigs Don't Fly' about these episodes, which over the decades inspired so many little vignettes and ideas, and the title of an old forgotten B-side 'This World Needs A Father' came directly from one such addled foray. 'Where The Pigs Don't Fly' was my attempt to marry the mundane with the surreal in the vein of Barrett-era Floyd; the references to 'stolen ice-cream vans' and kids covering their jumpers in roses were little snippets of childhood memories which I planted within the song's wobbly, trippy framework. The original slightly inept version that I wrote on my old Aria Elecord was much quirkier and frailer than the version that made it into the studio, which was somehow more robust and seventies-sounding. The line 'Where the pigs don't fly, I do' was I suppose an attempt to sum up how perverse it felt stumbling through the dreary suburban streets in an utterly altered state, the manicured order of the everyday world reduced to a strange and laughable mirage.

Once we even managed to get hold of some acid: strange illicit little squares of blotting paper printed with a fingerprint-shaped dose of LSD. Joining us was a boy who would become my lifelong friend — the picaresque and often hilarious Alan Fisher. It was a beautiful summer's day in the mid-eighties and we had drifted up to Beechhurst, a kind of gentle, old-fashioned, suburban amusement park with a bowling green, miniature railway and pitch-and-putt course sat on the outskirts of the town. It was, incidentally, where my parents had held their wedding reception a generation earlier, and it was the setting for one of the oddest and most memorable afternoons of my life as the three of us stumbled for hours around the miniature golf course, shaking with laughter, the point of the game forgotten as groups of frail grannies gazed on in amused confusion, probably wondering what could possibly be that funny. Those were wonderful, wonderful times when the future stretched out limitless and unchained, dappled with possibility, and like all young people we thought we were immortal and that those times would last for ever.

Simon's story was later to unfold as a tragedy, however. He became depressed in his early twenties and ended up taking his own life. Those hazy, sun-kissed days with him would become all the more poignant as the years rolled on and he remained for ever the warm, lovely boy who wasn't to be. I went to his funeral back in Haywards Heath in the nineties with my father and managed to endure it quietly until the service ended with the Beatles' 'Let It Be'. As the beautiful, plaintive melody swelled and grew I was reminded of all the afternoons we had sat in his bedroom listening to the same song, and I finally lost my control and wept like a baby in my dad's arms. The lyrics to the song 'Breakdown' were written with him in mind and a decade later I tried in vain to do his memory some sort of justice with the song 'Simon', but I learned that the artifice of music can never quite describe something as complete as a person. It just ends up feeling like so many pretty words.

It was a strange, in-between sort of time. I was free from the grids and structures of school but still too young to grasp any tangible path, and I found myself coasting in a desultory way. I became sucked into a vaguely misogynistic, parochial world of underpowered motorbikes, minor shoplifting and drunken episodes on village greens. My friend Simon Cambers and I both managed to scrape some money together to buy cheap, third-hand Yamaha DT 50s, and we would whizz and splutter around the ring roads and roundabouts of Haywards Heath, flouting traffic laws and causing concern. Our favourite trick was to wear Spiderman or Mr T masks underneath our bike helmets and overtake cars and watch the shocked, confused expression of the drivers as we swivelled our heads round to face them. I was usually dressed in an old sixties black biker's jacket that my dad had given me, on the back of which I'd written *Lou Reed* in white paint, and my hair-cut was a homemade effort I'd stupidly effected in front of the mirror one ill-advised evening. I was aiming for a severe, punkish sort of crop but ended up looking wretched and patchy like a cancer patient or an escapee from a laboratory. Unbelievably, in those days young men were able to drive reasonably powerful motorbikes with absolutely no test or training. I was an utterly awful driver with zero road sense and no appreciation of how to maintain my bike, so it came as no surprise to anyone when I eventually smashed it into a wall after trying to overtake a car on a bend in the rain with bald tyres and very nearly killed myself. The ribbons of permanent scars that still wind up my legs are always a harsh reminder of my blithe, youthful recklessness. I think that during this whole period I was exploring my limits and thresholds in the way that young men do, challenging myself in an attempt to emulate what I perceived masculinity to be; a vision that was being passed down to me through the usual channels but distorted by the overtly laddish culture of my drab satellite town. Before I had the maturity and confidence to become myself, I think, I was playing around with the idea of becoming someone else; trying on the clothes that didn't really suit me and developing those brittle layers, that fragile emotional shell that many men wear all their lives as they strive to become an almost fictional construct – an amalgamation of other people's traits garnered from idols and parents and peers.

One summer, in an ill-advised moment of youthful enthusiasm, Simon Cambers and I decided to embark on a cheap holiday together. We chose Ibiza as there were rumours of riotous times to be had, which appealed to our wide-eyed teenage quest for adventure and encounter. Unfortunately, we found ourselves in San Antonio, a sort of grim 18–30 safari park, a microcosm of all the worst elements of low-cost Britain complete with kebab shops and pubs called the Red Lion, and awash with lager and roaming gangs of desperate, agitated, single young men from Kettering. On the first night, Simon became dehydrated after an evening of boozing and drank some tap-water to quench his thirst only to spend the next ten days in bed rolling around groaning and clutching his stomach as the gastro-enteritis he had developed worked its way through his body. For the rest of the holiday I wandered alone around the grotty, vomit-washed streets, disconnected and melancholy and wing-manless, locked in a Martin Parr hell of 'Choose Life' T-shirts and fried breakfasts, the heady promise of reckless, jolly escapades reduced to a bitter fantasy spotlit by the cold reality of my teenage diffidence as I found myself unable to mingle or meet. Ironically, decades later, the real beauty of the island would reveal itself as my wife introduced me to the quiet rural calm of the north where we would spend endless pampered, panting summers; the island's other saltier side a strange and distant shadow.

Back in Haywards Heath, another term started at college, and once all the students had gone home I would wander down to the caretaker's smoky cubby-hole of a room to collect my bucket of sprays and cloths, and go about my evening job: cleaning the college's toilets, changing the loo rolls, filling the soap dispensers and mopping the tiled floors. Writing about it now, it probably comes across as unpleasant and demeaning, but I don't remember it that way. I was just pleased to be making some money, and anyway it wasn't slave labour; most of the time I'd sit around chatting, smoking roll-ups and drinking weak, milky tea with the caretaker – a wiry, tough, likeable ex-sailor with a sleeve of blurry blue tattoos, a severe hair-cut and an arsenal of anecdotes.

There was an industrial estate near the college and I managed to get a job there one summer in a factory called Worcester Valve. It was a bleak, depressing sort of place full of shuffling, spent, middle-aged men who seemed to pass the whole day complaining and leering at tabloids. I was given a hammer and shown outside to a huge pile of industrial valves. My job was to individually break off a little protruding metal arm from each of them and then throw the armless ones into a new pile. By the end of the summer the pile had shifted a few metres and I had spent every single moment of every single day performing the same dull, numbing task. It left me yearning for my mop.

There was another boy who I started to notice at college. He was very tall and strangely fascinating despite a kind of gauche Gothiness. I would notice him holding court in the sour-smelling common room, an audience of wide-eyed acolytes huddled around him hanging on his every word as he enlightened them about the nuances of Marxism or proportional representation. His presence was magnetic and compelling, and one day I wandered in to find him sitting alone playing some post-punk riff on an old bass guitar and started talking to him about music. His name was Mat Osman. I was a bit wary of him at first – he'd arrived at college via the posher rival school, Warden Park, with which Oathall was predictably locked in pointless, violent, endless feuds. His obvious sophistication and intelligence could be intimidating; he was able to discuss politics and culture with what seemed like great skill, and voicing opinion as fact he had a confidence bordering on arrogance. I decided I liked him. My earliest memory of Mat is as a kind of inchoate political firebrand; he organised a student protest about something or other, getting the whole college to evacuate the building en masse and sit down outside. As the principal, obviously well versed in the psychology of crowd control, picked off individuals and threatened them with suspension, the protest began to crumble. Mat was the only one with the wherewithal to realise that strength lay in unity so he shouted out, 'Everyone stay sitting down – he can't suspend us all!' If his threatened expulsion had actually materialised I might not be sitting here writing this. He was principled and cultured in a way I hadn't experienced before, which was exciting and inspiring, and I decided that there was a lot that I could learn from him.

By this point, in a kind of ill-advised Dylanesque homage, I'd taken to busking folk songs around Haywards Heath. I'd stand outside Sainsbury's in South Road with Simon Holdbrook bawling out inept versions of 'With God On Our Side' or 'The Wreck Of The Edmund Fitzgerald' until we were moved on or, as was more usual, paid a few coins to stop. One day I brought my guitar to college, and Mat overheard my tuneless fumbling and asked me to join his band. They were called Paint It Black and they needed a guitar player, so I joined them in one of those pre-fab modular Portakabins found on school and college grounds the world over, and we ran through a series of simple derivative pieces. In my experience there's always a thrill in playing music with other people;

it's a kind of willing self-deception that lulls you into a pleasurable trance which often belies the objective quality of what you're actually doing. Hence the existence of so many awful bands ploughing on under the illusion that they are creating something extraordinary. We were no different, but the experience must have given us some sort of momentum as we stumbled gamely on and organised more rehearsals.

There was this local boy who Mat knew called Gareth Perry. He had a reputation as a handsome lothario, and as his brother was a famous model – the toned hunk holding the baby in the ubiquitous black and white eighties poster – he had a certain parochial mystique. Such proximity to the distant corridors of fame and glamour was certainly intoxicating to us small-town wannabes, but more importantly he could actually sing. He had a strong, *X-Factor* judge-pleasing soul/pop sort of voice and an obvious presence, so he ended up being our front man. For some reason we would often rehearse at my house, all crammed into my dank, north-facing bedroom with my Pink Floyd mural and my collage of strange photos. Perched on my single bed we would plough enthusiastically through our repertoire of five-chord songs with predictable titles like 'She's The Knife' or 'Reasons For Leaving', while my dad continually interrupted trying to interest us in pictures of Chopin's death mask or his new book about Elgar. The harsh censure that he'd reserved for my previous band seemed to have eased somewhat, possibly because he seemed to believe that Mat was, at least superficially, some sort of reincarnation of Franz Liszt. Indeed, in one of the many portraits of the composer that hung on the walls the likeness was uncanny, both sharing the same hawkish profile and distant, imperial countenance. Mat politely answered and reanswered the barrage of questions about his family's heritage, but my dad refused to be any less fascinated by him. Anyway, we soldiered on with the rock-by-numbers repertoire for a while until slowly the Zeitgeist began to bleed in.

During the mid-eighties, spearheaded by bands like The Smiths, alternative music was challenging the tenets of rock and starting to invert the posturing of the seventies. Songs about weakness and failure and the drudgery of real life began to resonate powerfully with me, and inspired by the *C86* movement and the shambling bands we renamed ourselves Geoff. Its ridiculous, comic ordinariness appealed to us as a kind of wry celebration of the prosaic. We all started dressing in an unofficial uniform: tight turned-up jeans and big shoes and odd, dark-blue denim factory-workers' jackets that looked like truncated lab coats. We would trudge down to Brighton every now and then to stand smoking in a winding queue with all the other fashion victims, waiting to receive our £2.50 box-cuts in a barber's by the station called Freddy's. The look was very much inspired by the eighties student fashion for aping the iconography of socialism, but I think we believed, in a probably misguided way, that we'd introduced our own twist. I part-exchanged my old, red, Westone Thunder 1-Active electric guitar for a cheap semi-acoustic 335 copy in a vain attempt to sound more like Johnny Marr, and we chiselled away at our sound. Unfortunately, as the lead guitarist I simply wasn't technically a good enough musician to pull it off, and the songs that we thought were starting to sound a bit like 'Cemetery Gates' were probably actually sounding more like 'Happy Hour'. Nevertheless, we achieved some minor local attention as exponents of what the town rag called 'Bedroom Rock' and we would 'gig' exclusively, you've guessed it, in people's bedrooms, inviting a paltry, disinterested audience who would mutter through the songs and feign enthusiasm when we finished.

Sometimes Mat and I would write stuff at his house. Despite a patina of middle-classness, his beginning wasn't much grander than my own. He and his brother Richard had been brought up in a similarly boxy little house in a similarly depressing part of Haywards Heath by his single teacher mother. Although his family was much better educated than mine, it was still trapped in the same sort of grim lower echelons of the British class system: baked beans for tea and the stale fug of paraffin heaters. Richard was a bit younger and, although now always fault-lessly charming, I remember him as being comically grumpy. One afternoon we were sitting in Mat's room listening to *Forever Changes* when Richard suddenly barged in and shouted '*The sixties were rubbish and Love are rubbish!*' and then stormed out again in a cloud of stroppy, teenage righteousness.

The band stumbled on for a while, but without any proper gigs booked, and once the initial adrenal enthusiasm had worn off an inevitable inertia began to creep in. I think Gareth may have 'gone travelling' or something, and as university beckoned our interest in the band faded, the members cast adrift in different cities, the songs forgotten and the name nothing but an amusing footnote.

5

For my parents, I think higher education seemed like a distant, unfamiliar, slightly forbidding world where only the offspring of the privileged dare venture. They filled my life with a rich tapestry of art and music and books and beauty, but apart from a few chats with my sister I was forced to navigate the formal channels of schooling alone and unmentored. There wasn't much effective careers advice from my college either, so I found myself studying subjects that bored me and was left with qualifications that seemed irrelevant. When it came to applying to university the only vaguely arts-oriented course

I could do with science and maths A-levels was something called Town and Country Planning, for which I was accepted at Manchester. Looking back, my choice of city was very much influenced by the music that I was listening to. I'd fallen in love with the Fall's wiry surrealism – records like *This Nation's Saving Grace* and *The Wonderful and Frightening World* had become almost sacred to me – and I had worn my stylus down to a nub playing Joy Division's *Unknown Pleasures*. Meanwhile, The Smiths' colossal shadow of influence was ever growing; theirs was such a unique place in the world of pop – cultish and still distinctly marginal but with the reach to make thrilling little forays into the mainstream, so being a fan felt just as transgressive as being into the Pistols years earlier. They had hovered around my consciousness until one solitary evening when I was listening to Peel on late-night Radio 1 and heard Johnny Marr's gnawing, insistent guitar hook coming through my tiny transistor speaker and Morrissey's saturnine promise of leaping in front of a flying bullet, and that was it for me. Theirs was a truly special chemistry, at once familiar but unique, a perfectly balanced dance between jangly conceit and pitch-black humour that held me enthralled for years.

The eloquent paeans to the confusions and complexities of life resonated powerfully with my teenage self, and I felt their pull dragging me further in as I trudged around Manchester's wintry tarmacked streets. My choice of city had been another highly idealistic decision on my part. I had a very romanticised vision of what living there would be like and imagined some sort of gritty crucible of bohemian creativity where I would meet a pool of like-minded musicians, when in reality life within the student community felt somehow soulless and disconnected as I struggled to meet anyone with whom I felt much kinship. I loved the city's hard, post-industrial edge but life there quickly began to feel testing, and I grew tired of the gaggles of over-excited toga-draped pranksters who roamed the corridors of Owen's Park, the huge, forbidding, nineteen sixties hall of residence I'd ended up in, unable and unwilling to summon up the enthusiasm required to join their shrill, drunken games. One of the few pools of light in the gloom was a fellow planner called Dave McGuire with whom I had become close. He was a shrewd, friendly, hulking redhead from Darlington who shared the same taste in music and had a similarly sour slant, and who for some reason called everyone 'Wilf'.

We would buy bottles of fortified wine called Night Train Express and trudge up Oxford Road to the union to attend cheap gigs – groups like The Weather Prophets, The Bodines and all of those *C86* outfits that filled the post-Smiths' break-up landscape – and stand at the bar in our second-hand turned-up 501s with our subsidised lager trying to look heedless and inscrutable while the bands thrashed away.

This was back when if you were from a 'disadvantaged' family you could claim a full grant so, as well as my fees, my accommodation and paltry living expenses were also paid for. The truth was I hadn't yet developed expensive tastes so during weekends there I would just buy a loaf of bread and eat Marmite on toast for breakfast, lunch and dinner, chomping away as I listened enraptured to *The Hounds of Love* or *The Queen Is Dead* on the same crappy Boots Audio record player I'd dragged up from Haywards Heath, the Pennine rain pounding against the pavement eighteen floors below. Other weekends I'd pick up my brown paper-bagged, vegetarian-takeaway breakfast from the hall canteen and scurry over to Chorlton Street coach station. I'd sit munching my hard-boiled egg on the National Express travelling down the M1 to Victoria from where I would get a train back to Sussex to visit Alex Goldman, the inevitable small-town sweetheart with whom I was conducting a fraught, failing, long-distance relationship. We'd met at college where I'd been ensnared by her crimped, lacquered hair-do and her obvious feminine wiles, and we had been locked into the usual teenage pact of lust and recrimination for a while. She lived with her kind, sweet parents at the time in a comfortable bungalow in Burgess Hill. I was staying there that famous night of the great storm of 1987 when an oak tree toppled and fell across the house snapping the central beam and stopping a few feet from my head. If the door in the room in which I was staying had not been closed and given extra support I'm told the tree would have crashed through the lintel and crushed my skull like an egg-shell. I just remember being savagely snatched from my sleep by a hellish, screaming sound and reaching up to feel wet oak leaves and bark just above my head, and crawling out, fuelled by fear and instinct, through the broken glass accompanied by the flash of torches and shouts of panic and confusion. Apparently I insisted on finding my socks first. Well, one should always be properly dressed.

While I was nearly being killed by trees or strug-gling around Rusholme pretending I was in a John Osborne play, back in Haywards Heath my mother had been waiting patiently to leave my father. Like most people of their generation my parents had mar-ried far too young. They were still essentially almost kids themselves when they committed to each other back in the early sixties, and after the romance and the thrill of infatuation had faded, and the disori-enting fog of child-rearing had cleared, they were starkly confronted with each other, raw and real in the unforgiving daylight; two people who despite some shared experience actually had little in common and who inevitably over the years had begun the slow, cold, lonely drift towards estrangement. I think my father had made that fatal old mistake of taking her for granted, and certainly his language towards her over the years had merged into disrespectful, unflat-tering nicknames and lazy in-jokes, which replaced any previous tenderness or kindness and betrayed a numbing of his feeling towards her. Their twenty-five years together had followed the well-trodden path from infatuation to indifference with all the points in-between and had slowly shifted into a joyless, grinding war of attrition. They might have loved each other at one point but I'm not sure if they ever actually really liked each other, and when passion fades where there is no fondness or respect there is sometimes little else to hold things together. My mother had selflessly endured his ever-darkening moods, cutting asides and bleak frustrations in that old-fashioned way that parents did in those days 'for the good of the children'. I admire her flinty stoicism but feel sad that she must have been so unhappy for so many years. My father was utterly, utterly destroyed, however, having had absolutely no suspicion that anything was amiss; his fragile world shattered when he came home from the taxi rank one day to find her things gone and her stark little letter sat on the mantelpiece. He had built a wall of fantasy around himself, at the core of which was the myth that his wife was happy and that their marriage was still working. The regular unkindnesses he visited on her must have been alien to this fiction so he chose to ignore them. Even years after she left him he would wallow in this denial, telling me how people often remarked that they 'were always holding hands' or something similarly sugary. His infuriating arrogance often reminded me of Dalí's famous improbable elephants with the impossibly spindly legs; the fragile structure of his reality always at the point of buckling under the weight of his grandiose self-deception. But behind it all, of course, was hiding a small and frightened man, and as his life fell apart I was filled with sadness and an impulse to help. I decided to leave Manchester, mainly to spend time with him and help sweep up the shattered pieces, but also admittedly because I was finding student life there dull. I moved back to my cramped little bedroom in Haywards Heath and made my dad tea and listened through the walls as he shuffled around his tiny broken kingdom and sobbed himself to sleep. There were endless stale weeks peppered with fraught, angry episodes that dissolved into puddles of pity, boil-in-the-bag dinners and glum hours trudging around the nature reserve or sat listening to Chopin, but slowly he began to be able to face the day and I thought it was time for me to move on.

Mat was studying at the LSE and living in a flat in a handsome mansion block in Ridgmount Gardens just by Goodge Street station. There was a spare bed there, so using the money I'd scraped together temping in dull offices in Haywards Heath I moved in for a few weeks while I decided what to do with my life. It was only really a one-bedroom flat but there were six of us: three girls in the bedroom, and Mat, his friend Ade and me in separate, narrow, single beds in the living room. In the day I'd waft around the capital, eating salad kebabs, sitting for hours on the Circle Line or window-shopping in the maze of electronics shops along Tottenham Court Road, and in the evening we would drift off into pot-babble and listen to music and chatter and giggle into the small hours of the morning. It became a sort of ritual for us boys to fall asleep to The Pet Shop Boys' 'Rent', a clever, beautiful poem of nineteen eighties city life that I still adore and which never fails to remind me of those first wonderful days when I began to fall in love with London.

During this whole period I'd carried on writing songs, and while I had been in Manchester had recorded them on my primitive Fostex 4-Track and sent cassette tapes to Mat in London. We would play this hilarious game where I was the 'artist' and he assumed the role of 'journalist', and would send me back in-depth critiques framed as *NME* reviews complete with marks out of ten. I still own one of

them, and the sweet, callow tone of the accompanying letter always makes me feel wistful for a time
when we were still young men, when our relationship
was still uncoloured by the endless dead hours spent
in airports and dressing rooms, and by the stresses
and frictions of career and money and the chase for
success. He was always unrealistically positive. The
songs, with titles like 'Empty House' and 'Somewhere
Along The Way', which I hoped sounded a bit like
Felt or The Loft, actually sounded weak and tuneless,
but he would receive them in the spirit of friendship
as minor masterpieces, and in my self-mythologising
way I would be happy to almost believe him. So we
continued to dabble and potter. I'm not sure if either
of us knew where we thought it was going to lead.

I began to coast around, staying with different
people in different parts of the country. My old friend
Alan was living with his sister down in Mitcham in
south London. They had some space on their sofa so I
ended up staying there for a while, living on baguettes
and humous from the nearby Safeway supermarket.
This was the era of Terence Trent D'Arby and Bros,
and as Alan had a twin brother and they were both
blonde and handsome they had unwisely begun to ape

that awful eighties style, something for which I would savagely take the piss. I'll always remember that Alan had a shoe-box full of photographs of his life, most of which, bizarrely, seemed to be shots of his ex-girlfriends naked and crying. I could never wheedle out of him how he'd managed to regularly orchestrate situations that simultaneously seemed to involve elements of sexuality, voyeurism and grief. I've always thought that if he had been slightly more inclined towards an arty sort of intellectualism they would have made the basis of a fascinating exhibition. When Alan wasn't working we would take the tube up to Hampstead and hang around with a gang of rent boys that we had met through his brother. For some reason we called them The Hampstead Muffins, and they lived like a little family in bleak-looking social housing hidden well away from the quaint and pretty Georgian village. Most of them were runaways from places like rural Wales, and to supplement their dole cheques would dabble in a bit of minor dealing and sell us cheap trips. They were a hilarious and strangely inspiring bunch – flamboyant and funny and utterly inclusive. We spent several afternoons with them parading in altered states around the plush and

moneyed streets, giggling uncontrollably and pirou-
etting on bins and swinging like scruffy Gene Kellys
around the lamp-posts while the well-heeled mums
gazed quizzically on.

I went back to Manchester for a while, moving in
with a girl I'd met at university called Emily, who was
from Middlesbrough. She was a confident, warm, fun
girl who loved music and studied chemistry and lived
in a flat in Daisybank Road in Longsight. I stayed
with her and her flat-mate and made tea and got in
the way and listened to Ian Dury and Kate Bush, and
wrote a song about her called 'Just A Girl'. It's the
oldest song I have written ever to be released and it
sat around for years until one day I was forced to raid
my bottom drawer for a B-side and remembered it.
To be honest, it's a terrible steal of an old country song
my parents used to play, but it showed some understanding for storytelling and melody, and still actually
moves me in some simple, probably nostalgic way.
The line about the 'ashtray eyes and boot-lace ties'
was a reference to Ian Dury's 'Sweet Gene Vincent',
a song we used to play until the grooves wore out,
and the picture it paints of two young people fumbling around the beginnings of feeling set against the

back-drop of an unfamiliar city's coal-black winter still manages to stir something in me and takes me back to a sweet forgotten corner of my youth.

Looking for work one day in the local job centre, I saw advertised amongst the sea of vacancies at call centres and thinly disguised positions as sex workers a job as a DJ in a local nightspot. It was a place called the Cyprus Tavern, a sticky-floored, subterranean cellar bar on Princess Street, which was at the time home to frightening packs of football fans and herds of belligerent single young men pointedly looking for trouble. It smelled of stale smoke and bleach and spilled beer, and was the sort of place where no one planned to end the evening. I pretended that I'd had experience and was thrown in the deep end one Saturday night armed with a clutch of Freda Payne and Roxy Music records. The bouncers had told me that if I spotted a fight on the dance-floor I should stop the music as a sign for them to march down and break up the tussle. My inexperience and ineptitude meant that my 'set' was always peppered with gaps as I fiddled away inexpertly and frantically with the equipment. Hearing the silences and taking them as their cue the bouncers would rush down to the dance-floor, their eyes darting around looking for the phantom trouble-makers, while the meagre crowd would sigh and mutter. I gradually gained a little competence and confidence, and started to arrogantly replace the Phyllis Nelson records with more left-field stuff, much to the chagrin of some of the punters. One night, after ignoring a request to play some reggae record, I was followed home and chased down Plymouth Grove by a gang of lads of who had taken offence, forcing me to sprint into the grounds of a nearby school and hide cowering in one of the industrial bins while they stormed around drunkenly baying for satisfaction. My *Slumdog Millionaire*-style twenty minutes in a vat of banana skins and old yoghurt pots probably saved me from a week in hospital, and years later the experience would inform the lyrics to 'Killing Of A Flash Boy'; a song inspired by the random small-town violence I saw on every street, the threats of brutish thuggery and the terrifying near misses like this and countless others. The eponymous 'flash boy' was myself – the eternal prey, the fated quarry, hair gelled and coiffed, marked and targeted and 'asking for it'.

As the year ebbed away and September rolled around again, I parted on good terms with Manchester, a hard, beautiful city full of proud people for which I still have so much fondness, but its damp, wind-blown streets never really felt like home and I drifted back to the dazzle and spin of London.

6

My time wafting around Bloomsbury had rekindled my love for the capital. It all started many years before in childhood when during the odd weekend or half-term my family would jump on the train up to Victoria and then on to the Circle Line to South Kensington in order to 'visit the museums'. The rattle and drone of tube stations, and that peculiar dusty, diesel smell still gives me a slight frisson, and when I felt trapped in the cage of my dreary town as a kid I would often just walk to Haywards Heath railway station to stand on the platform and wistfully look northwards up the tracks trying to glimpse some of the lustre and promise beyond. There's something about the size of London I find comforting: the sense of anonymity, the wealth, the power, the possibility. All the love and poison indeed.

I was accepted on a Town Planning course at UCL, and with Mat and a motley collection of other students moved into a large, crumbling Victorian house on Wilberforce Road in Finsbury Park. In order to minimise rent the whole house was crammed with beds, so the only communal space was the mildewy, laminated MDF kitchen where we would gather and stand around chatting and chomping on toast. It opened out on to a small, scruffy, weed-strewn garden where no one ever went, not even in summer. It was basically a dumping ground crowded with old fridges and pots of dried-up paint and a tangle of broken furniture. The only warmth in the house came from those rattly old Calor-gas heating units with heavy orange cylinders which we would have to haul up and down the stairs. Their cosy, gassy smell still reminds me of those days. Mat's, Ade's and my rooms were right at the top of the house, so we effectively lived in our own separate little enclave away from the other sub-tribes that had inevitably sprung up through the forces of the house geopolitics. Below us, in the master bedroom, there was a kind of alpha-male Goth called Colin and his henchman Dan, who were both also at LSE but who didn't really bother climbing up the stairs very often, so Mat, Ade and I would often spend the evening together in the same giggly, fuddled haze of dope and chatter and music that we had in Ridgmount Gardens. I remember we would sit on the beds in our coats, huddled around the heater, smoking and cracking pistachio nuts while we listened to records like Felt's 'Space Blues' or 'Solid State Soul' by Raymonde, the carpet of shells scattering and spreading across the lino.

Anyone who knows London will understand that living in Finsbury Park is very different from living in Fitzrovia, but I loved the scruffy streets and the kebab houses and the shops full of cheap plastic tat that were precursors to the Pound stores. I've always been inspired by the arse-end of the city and tried to look for stories and vignettes in the bustle and majesty of the everyday. I would wander around in my ridiculous fantasy paying all of these images into the growing bank of song ideas I kept in my notebooks, scribbling down phrases that I overheard on the Underground or copying graffitied scrawlings that I came across in the toilet cubicles. Songs like 'She' and 'This Time' and 'By The Sea' and 'My Insatiable One' and 'Sound Of The Streets' and countless, countless others that mention the 'nowhere places' and the hinterlands and the cashpoints and the escalators – were born from these outings as I slowly pieced together a kind of Impressionist collage from the flotsam and debris that littered the streets of the capital; a lexicon torn from the dirty pulse of the city.

As another way to explore London sometimes Mat and I would play something we invented called The Dice Game. Very much influenced by the Luke Rhinehart book, we would go to a tube station and throw dice to choose a line, and then throw again to choose the number of stops and take the train that the roll of chance had determined. At the designated station we would get out and buy something relevant: a little model of Big Ben at Westminster, a West Ham mug at Upton Park etc. etc. Of course, in reality it meant that we came back home laden with an armful of *Neasden Gazette*s and *Perivale Chronicle*s as most places didn't have landmarks or stadiums to their names, but the point of the game was really that there was no point beyond the adventure itself. I'd always found names like Dollis Hill and Seven Sisters and Hounslow evocative and intriguing and strangely exotic, and wondered why the romance for place names in music seemed to be reserved exclusively for destinations like Wichita and Chattanooga. Once I had grasped a little of the skill of painting detail I would set songs within very particular areas of London and, even if I didn't always use the place name in the lyric itself, the technique would help bring the song to life for me and hopefully that sense would be passed on to the listener. 'Asphalt World' was a complex tale of three-way sexual jealousy set specifically in Highgate and in the endless cab journeys spent shuttling back and forth along the Archway Road. 'By The Sea' was a story of escape from Seven Sisters on the nether reaches of the Victoria Line, and Sadie, the fictional flaneuse of 'She' and 'Sound Of The Streets' roamed the sun-kissed pavements of North Kensington, wearing out her shoe leather on Chesterton Road and Ladbroke Grove. The use of such minutiae in writing would be something that I would ruminate on often over the years; the way if used right it could locate the narrative so neatly and breathe life into the words. I began to eschew the cliché about writing about universal experiences as I tried to do the exact opposite, convinced that the most powerful resonance was achieved through focusing on the microscopic rather than the macroscopic. I wanted to record the world I saw around me, real, and uncomfortable and up close: the blue plastic bag caught in the branches of the tree, the clatter and rumble of the escalator – London in all of its wonderful, shitty detail.

I arrived at UCL in 1987, studying at the Bartlett School of Architecture and Planning on Gower Street. I suppose to be honest like many kids at that age I was just still drifting, and I certainly had little interest in my course beyond it allowing me to delay life. There were so few planners that we were thrown in with the architects. One of them started to catch my eye. She was extremely beautiful in an almost Middle Eastern or Mediterranean way with long unwashed dark hair cut in a severe fringe. She would always wear scruffy clothes like faded, vintage Mickey Mouse T-shirts or big clumpy biker's boots, but somehow they just managed to make her look more elegant and moneyed. There was a student cafe on Gower Street called the Crypt or something, and one day I was sitting with my cup of tea and she came over to me and started talking. The first thing I noticed up close was that she had brown, discoloured teeth and what I thought at first was a speech impediment. Through her nervous, lisping drawl I managed to make out that her name was Justine. Justine Frischmann. We had a field trip the next week to the Weald and Downland Open Air Museum near Chichester and she made me some sandwiches to eat on the coach. It was such a simple, touching gesture, and it was the beginning of one of the two great loves of my life. We started hanging around together, although I'm not quite sure what she saw in a gauche, provincial twig like me. My naive parochial charm must have been novel to her. She, however, was so urbane and worldly that I'm surprised I never found her daunting. For me she somehow exuded London – the wealth, the power and indeed the possibility – but her confidence never stepped over into arrogance as she possessed a clumsy, disarming kind of charm that seduced everyone she met. She was the sort of person in whose presence everyone felt special; completely aware of her obvious lures but at the same time oddly detached from them.

She was extremely powerful and I think she knew it. The reason I found her voice unusual at first was because I'd never really come across an accent that was the product of an expensive education before. Her father was an extremely successful engineer and her upbringing had been littered with the kind of luxury and privilege that I could only guess at. In order to spend more time bathing in her light I switched my degree course to Architecture and we began a gentle, hazy and at first fairly innocent relationship, the kind that wears the mask of affectionate friendship but that hides a secret, carnal truth. The first project we were assigned was to design a pergola in Gordon Square. We would wander there from The Bartlett and sit on one of the park benches in the October sunshine, and I would listen to her soft, lilting drawl as the conversation spooled and fragmented, and I tried not to stare at her too much. There were never any limits with Justine – she was always fascinated and fascinating, wise yet humble, intellectual yet earthy, murky and thoughtful, yet silly and joyous and wonderfully playful. I have a photo of one of those days – the first photo ever taken of us together. In it we are being deliberately melodramatic and studied, but the sepia wash and alabaster skin tones somehow accidentally capture an idealised truth of those precious first moments. She taught me how to gain pleasure from being near beautiful things or from simple combinations of colours, she taught me about modernism and how to appreciate spaces, and she introduced me to a host of unfamiliar artists from Ingres to Allen Jones, but she would never lecture and never monologue, and all the while had a slightly lascivious smile playing across what she called her 'sea monster lips'. One evening after a late night at college she came back to Wilberforce Road and we laid around for hours smoking and talking and eating nuts by the gas fire and eventually fell asleep listening to the rain outside. In the morning when Mat met her for the first time I remember feeling so proud of both of them, in their own different ways such wonderful people that had become so dear to me and that I had brought together. Justine became almost a resident of Wilberforce Road, and would often lean against the Formica worktop in the kitchen in her grey woollen Joseph dress charming everyone and chewing on her salad kebab while talking about Walter Gropius politely between mouthfuls. One December night, however, towards Christmas 1987 when the house had been pretty much emptied of students for the holidays, she turned up on my doorstep and we jabbered and chattered deep into the coal black morning, and by the time we woke up again the next day our relationship had changed for ever.

She lived with her two cats in a luxury one-bedroom flat in another handsome mansion block, this time on Hornton Street in Kensington just opposite the hulking, Brutalist town hall. I began to stay there so regularly that it seemed like I had virtually moved in, and we would shuttle backwards and forwards from Kensington to Finsbury Park so often that even the route became synonymous with her. Even years later when I drive through Maida Vale and along Abercorn Place and over Abbey Road towards St John's Wood I'm reminded of those endless hours sat in her little off-white Renault smoking and listening to cassette tapes on the car stereo, and talking about the lyrics to 'Cygnet Committee'. London became endlessly fascinating to me as I slowly unpeeled its secrets. There was this bit of graffiti on a wall in Marble Arch which I noticed one day and that we both began to love saying simply *Modern Life is Rubbish* in stark white letters. We drove past it countless times and it never failed to fascinate us; bold and shocking and completely unexpected against the faded grey of the city. Her flat was elegantly corniced, high ceilinged and full of the hallmarks of wealth – gilt mirrors, fine furniture and a hefty television – but in the bedroom next to the futon there stood a little vintage Dansette turntable and a stack of old records; mainly easy listening albums like Stan Getz and Astrid Gilberto, or folk-rock classics like Van Morrison and Joni Mitchell, nothing particularly challenging or contemporary. Justine may have taught me about art but I introduced her to the kind of music that would end up defining her. She'd never heard of the Fall or the Happy Mondays before I met her, but her natural curiosity for the outré and her thirst to soak up interesting left-field culture led her to fall in love with every ragged beat. The pupil/teacher dynamic was reversed, and I loved playing her things like 'Reel Around the Fountain' or 'Primitive Painters' for the first time and watching her eyes widen as the thrill of discovery washed over her. In a borrowed flush of my father's arrogance I remember telling her to forget that dusty old seventies vinyl, that from now on *this* was the only music we were going to be listening to.

We found ourselves shuttling along within a comfortable groove; from High Street Kensington we would catch the Circle Line to Euston Square and wander along to Gower Street to attend lectures, which I began to find fascinating. Architecture is such a varied discipline, so one moment we would be learning about Émile Durkheim or Jasper Johns or the work of Mies Van Der Rohe, and the next we would be in life classes drawing nudes. Mine were always a bit rubbish compared to Justine's far more practised efforts; the only training I had had being those long winter nights back at home before we had a television, when Blandine, my mum and I would all sit and draw together, me cast as the blundering beginner always struggling to keep up with the standard of my mother and sister, who were both fine artists. After college we would shuffle back home through the chill of London with the commuters and the shoppers, and smoke and eat crumpets and lie for hours in the bath talking, or pad around the flat stroking the cats and listening to *Hatful of Hollow*. Justine would probably be the first to deny that she was a very accomplished guitarist but she could play a bit, and we would sometimes sit and strum together, and bash out clumsy versions of 'Heart Of Gold' or 'Letter To Hermione' until there was a buzz on the intercom and Mat would climb up the stairs and we would drink tea or play chess and smoke until the conversation descended into the inevitable late-night babble. She could sing a nice counterpoint though and we would often run through one of my old songs, 'Just A Girl', with her doing a passable Joan Baez impression. I had written another song called 'Justice', very much in debt to Aztec Camera's 'Oblivious' and other similarly jaunty acoustic outings, which we would all play together with Mat rumbling along on his old Fender Jazz bass. It had a basic grasp of melody and rhythm, and the beginnings of something that sounded like a song so we decided to record a proper demo, booking a short session at some cheap studio down in Brighton. The simple vocal/acoustic-electric guitar/bass and drum-machine recording obviously encouraged us, so we named ourselves The Perfect and pressed on writing more gentle *Lilac Time*-style musings with titles like 'Somebody's Daughter' and 'Vanity'. We even made a sleeve for the demo – a mysterious, shadowy picture Justine had taken of me in the flat – which we photocopied and used to make homemade cassette singles with our band name in a basic font, and we pressed them hopefully into the palms of those we misguidedly considered influential. With little feedback and safe within our bubble, we interpreted our efforts as minor masterpieces but the truth was they lacked any edge or depth or insight, or indeed any real musicality, and their shortcomings inevitably led to a lack of traction. Without the motor of momentum then our vague ambitions began to fade and crumble in the face of raw, hard reality.

Sometimes we would venture out of our cosy little world and dip our toes into the scurry and jostle of London clubland, eager to sample a little of the thrill and promise of youth. On Fridays we would go to a gay club called Heaven under the dank, gloomy arches on Charing Cross Road to mingle with the lovely wild-eyed boys and get lost in the pulse and rush of the rhythm, feeling its welling throb and the tingle of sweet abandonment. Or occasionally we'd drive to a migrating hippy club called Whirlygig that was sometimes held in Shoreditch Town Hall, famous for the parachute that would be draped over the crowd towards the end of the evening and the huddling groups of stoners and the little gangs of hippy kids who had been dragged along and forced to stay up way past their bedtimes. We would hang out and smoke and dance a bit but we always felt like observers, that it was never our world, merely our duty as young people to do the kind of thing we thought young people did.

One day at college I was called into the admin offices, sat down and told to call my mother. Since escaping from my dad she had moved up to a little village in the Lake District called Langwathby. I'd trekked up along the breath-taking Carlisle to Settle line a couple of times and stayed with her and her new chap in their little crofter's cottage nestled in the Cumbrian hills and we'd eaten baked potatoes and gone for walks, and I had watched her sketch as she listened to the radio, happy that she seemed to have found the quiet, rural life I think she had always craved. The number I had been given was for a hospital ward in the Penrith. Confused, I dialled the number and was told to wait, until eventually the phone was passed to my mum and over the crackly line she told me that she had been diagnosed with terminal cancer. To anyone who has yet to experience this kind of seismic news it's hard to explain how shocking and visceral it feels as the foundations of your world topple and spin; the sense of utter disbelief and the tides of rage and helplessness that follow. In a daze of bewilderment and denial I demanded to speak to the nurse, who baldly confirmed the grim news that my mother had less than six months to live.

The next day Justine and I took the train up to the Lake District and sat around Mum's cottage with Blandine for a few days, going over and over the same ground looking for a different answer, but always finding the same one. This was only going to end one way.

The initial shock began to fade, and we picked up our lives back in London and arranged for my mother to come and visit as at that point she seemed strangely sanguine. By the time she arrived, though, her appearance was shocking: heartbreakingly drawn and skeletal, and ravaged by chemotherapy. She was obviously extremely unwell. Even towards the end her stoicism was breath-taking having journeyed the hundreds of miles and struggled through the bustle of London when a lesser woman would have weakly taken to her bed. We fed her and made her as comfortable as we could, and I showed her a little of my life, but ignoring the elephant in the room we mainly sat with her, sipping tea and chatting, and I tried to somehow show her that the shy, dreamy child she was always a little worried about might actually be all right without her. Like any son I had loved my mother with a blind, primitive love, and like any mother she had spent her years in fealty to my needs – a lifetime of selflessly feeding and mending and comforting and caring that was about to end. The final moment our eyes ever met she was climbing into a taxi on Hornton Street, her sallow, once beautiful face smiling at me for the last time.

7

My mother's death almost destroyed me. I was unable to get out of bed for days and days, just shuffling to and from the toilet every few hours, the blinds drawn, the soft oblivion of the duvet waiting. I didn't eat and I didn't wash and I developed shingles: a nasty ring of angry spots around my midriff. I don't really remember much. I know I was at Justine's flat, and I suppose she must have sensitively carried on with life around me, but I really have no memory beyond lying crushed and motionless in her purple sheets as the traffic rushed past outside and the world marched on. I find the words hard to write and I know some people will frown at this, but I didn't go to the funeral – I was simply too devastated. I didn't see how some dry, formal, quasi-religious ceremony could possibly begin to represent my mum, that her memory was best kept alive by less tangible but more real means. I think I felt that being her son I didn't need to formally let the world know of my grief; that it was no one's business but my own – a private contract between her and me. Today I regret that massively, still looking for some sort of closure in lieu of my absence. Years after her death I tried to organise an informal marking of the place where her ashes were scattered on Mount Caburn in Sussex, but the closest I've come to publicly recognising it is in the form of the lyrics to the song 'The Next Life'. It's strange, but even at the time of writing it, it wasn't clear to me that it was about my mum, but songs are mysterious, sometimes shifting and changing and revealing themselves in different ways even to the writer. I've often found that when writing about an emotion – loss, for example – I'm unable to write about just one situation as parallel experiences and different people will poke their way into my head and form a sort of amalgam. Therefore, I've always found it a bit simplistic to discuss what a song is 'about' as the subject matter of a single song for me is often inspired by different things. The way I write is in many ways very instinctive and occasionally almost subconscious, like I'm not really in control of myself. I try to let my pen do the work before the brain gets too involved, and it's often only years later that I can pin any meaning on to it. I like this approach – it breathes life into the song. In the same way that oblique lyrics can be the most powerful, sometimes I find it boring to know what my own songs are about, and part of the thrill is working it out myself. And so it was with the lyrics of 'The Next Life' that I wrote as a general meditation on loss but that I realised years later were so crushingly obviously about my mother.

If there was anywhere I wanted to be during those coal black mornings after my mother's death, it was the bedroom in Hornton Street: a beautiful room at the back of the house away from the rumble and clatter of the traffic, and facing the gardens below with a huge picture window screened by a Roman blind. During happier times Justine and I would lie there together just listening to the peal of the bells coming from St Mary Abbotts Church, and then eventually emerge and ease into the day with coffee from the cafe on the corner, or a trip to The Muffin Man on Cheniston Gardens; a hilarious, old-fashioned, English tea house where we would sit and sip our Earl Grey, and try not to stare too much at the pompous, coiffured wealthy widows and their silly miniature dogs.

Slowly, then, I managed to find some ragged version of normality, and as the fog of grief began to clear I started to be able to listen to music again. One of the most valuable lessons I had learned from the tatty, homemade world of my childhood was that if you wanted something you made it yourself. Even though I didn't quite know what it was yet, the kind of music I wanted to listen to didn't seem to be out there and this was beginning to make me increasingly frustrated. One autumn evening Justine, Mat and I were watching *Top of the Pops* at the flat. I remember seeing some ridiculous, tired, hair-rock act dutifully going through their repertoire of priapic posturing, and thinking how shit it was, and saying something like, 'I just know we can do better than this'. The impetus from all of the seismic life changes I was experiencing must have shaken me out of my comfortable cocoon and filled me with a sense of *carpe diem*, so we decided to place an advert in the *NME* for a guitar player.

By this point Mat and I had officially moved out of Wilberforce Road, and I'd moved the few possessions that weren't at Justine's into a shared flat just opposite the roundabout at the top of Highlever Road in North Kensington. For anyone who doesn't know, North Kensington and Kensington are very different places; even though it's quite well-to-do now, in those days it was a slightly misleading name referring to the scruffy suburban badlands beyond the wrong bit of Ladbroke Grove. The flat ran to three bedrooms on the top floor of a tall Victorian house, but again had no communal area except the kitchen as we'd crammed it with tenants. It was blank and functional and slightly soulless with grey carpets and 'landlord magnolia' on the walls, not charmingly shabby like Wilberforce Road, but bleak and cheap in its own way. Our room was at the back with French windows that opened on to a lonely, disused, weed-strewn balcony, and in the other rooms hovered the usual random collection of rootless twentysomethings, including for a while Justine's rakish, funny school friend Geraldine, whose family home was across the library from her flat on

Campden Hill Road. Many years later, when we were writing *Coming Up*, Mat would move into a place on North Pole Road, just opposite Highlever Road, and in December would receive a sorry flood of children's Christmas requests and letters to Santa that had been addressed to *Number 1, The North Pole*. Effectively, the flat was just somewhere we stayed every now and then, and to be honest even though it was my room, Mat lived there more than I did, having just graduated and found himself in a kind of lumpen, desultory, post-degree fug. We would drive over in the Renault and Mat would be trudging around gloomily in his towelling dressing gown, eating Big Soup and scouring the Situations Vacant columns, and we would try to cheer him up. We kept our instruments there and a couple of amps, so that's where we decided to stage the 'auditions'. The ad was printed in a late 1989 edition of the *NME* with Debbie Harry on the cover. We deliberately chose the *NME* rather than *Melody Maker*, which was the traditional forum for this kind of thing, because in those days our idealism bordered on the quixotic and we wanted some sort of separation from the usual collection of jobbing musicians that tended to answer these kind of things.

The ad said something pompous and irritating like: *Guitarist wanted for inexperienced but important band. Influences – Smiths, Lloyd Cole, Bowie, Pet Shop Boys. No musos, no beginners. Some things are more important than ability.* Two people answered: the first was exactly the kind of identikit sleeveless-heavy-metal-T-shirted muso we'd hoped to avoid, and the second was a boy called Bernard Butler. I'd first suggested meeting him in a dodgy old man's pub I knew down on Ladbroke Grove called the Kensington Park, but when I'd asked how I would recognise him he'd wryly replied, 'Maybe I should wear a carnation', and I just gave him the address and told him to come over instead. Perhaps I'd already begun to romantically view the meeting as worthy of some sort of stage.

My first impression of Bernard as he hid behind a mop of thick, dark hair was that he was very quiet and very young, but that somehow despite his laconic replies and his callow appearance he didn't seem shy, just kind of contained and strangely confident. There was a sense that he was observing us and quietly weighing us up. I suppose we probably came across as three pretentious middle-class prats to him; our ideas certainly outstripped our meagre ability, and once tea had been drunk and etiquette had been observed, and we finally heard him play, the shocking quality of his musicianship exposed our ambition as the empty, groundless folly that it was. I've always found watching Bernard play so compelling, even under the dull forty-watt bulb of a rehearsal room, and away from the glare and glitter of the stage there is something intensely captivating about the way he gives himself so utterly to the music. It's an immersion that many others try to imply or imitate but one that Bernard completely owns. At once so violent and tender yet direct and purposeful, he was always, even from those first moments, such a very special talent. There's something of the skill and intensity of a surgeon in the way Bernard plays, like he's operating on the instrument so that anyone who is watching him falls into the same accepting state that a patient or an airline passenger inhabits— a kind of necessary, willing surrender into the hands of an expert. I realised very early on that if I wanted the accolades and the status I thought the world owed me then it was up to me to try to catch up with him. The only snippet of conversation I remember from that initial meeting was us telling him our age (I was just twenty-two at the time), and him turning round and starkly replying with something like, 'Well, you'd better get on with it then.' And he was right, we were too long in the tooth to still be ambitious dreamers sitting in bedrooms talking about it, and without meeting Bernard I'm sure that's exactly what we would have remained. It didn't all work perfectly at first, of course – the gap in ability took some time to bridge, and as with any band there needed to be a long period of frustration and failure before any chemistry was really revealed. Ours would actually feel longer than most but at first we were buoyed along by those early buds of enthusiasm, a sense that, to misquote Michelangelo, within the slab of marble there was a beautiful statue waiting to emerge if we could just find the right tools. The first original piece that Bernard played us was something called 'Miller Man'. I remember it being complex and melodic with an obvious stylistic nod to Johnny Marr and, indeed, The Smiths' writing dynamic became our model, with me trying to weld lyrics and melody on to Bernard's crammed, intricate opuses. Over those first few weeks he would present us with other flowing, labyrinthine, arpeggio-based pieces and I would struggle to do them justice. I was

yet to develop any real musical sense and too in thrall
to the dominance of words over melody but without
any real mastery of the skill of storytelling or the coup
de grâce of the killer hook.

So the weeks came and went. Bernard would
catch the tube to Ladbroke Grove and shuffle over
to Highlever Road with his Epiphone slung over his
back in its soft case, and in between our time spent
designing otiose community centres and libraries
that would never be built, we would hurry through
London and the chill of twilight to meet up and
run through our modest, growing repertoire. There
were songs with titles like 'So Liberated', 'Carry Me,
Marry Me', 'The Labrador In You' and 'Wonderful,
Sometimes': bitter pot-shots at the limitations of
class, clumsy addresses to latent sexuality and jaunty,
self-conscious love songs, all of them slightly tuneless and formless, and yet to possess any real bite or
drama. Thinking back with the cold, bleak light of
objectivity, there were also real limitations with my
voice. I had started my musical journey wanting to
be the quiet one at the back – the dutiful, strumming
sentinel hiding behind a Gretsch – but I just simply
wasn't good enough to play that role. As fate played

its hand I was ushered further forward, until one day I woke up blinking in the daylight to find myself cast as a singer in a band but lacking any real command over my instrument. It took a while for me to develop any power in my voice and for me to overcome my self-consciousness and inhibitions, and to embrace the violence and the madness and the river of feeling that one must in order really to be able to sing. To put it simply: the vocals were weak. But slowly, slowly through our failures we were learning and beginning to develop the ingredient that is the bed-rock of any half-decent collection of emerging musicians: cama-raderie. We started going to gigs together to carefully study the craft of other bands that were a few rungs above us. Whereas I chose to idealise and oversimplify music, Bernard understood more about the practical steps needed to construct the sound he had in mind and, like many guitar players, could be very technical and would carefully work on achieving this. Using money he had made from a part-time job at Rymans he slowly started building his collection of equip-ment and pedals, and began learning their nuances and variations. We wanted to shed the limp, acoustic sound of The Perfect so we invested in a second-hand drum machine, driving down the M4 to Feltham in the Renault one day to a forbidding-looking tower block under the Heathrow flight path and meeting up with some wild-eyed pill-head to swap about a hundred quid for an old Alesis HR-16. I remember getting it back to Justine's flat and being hypnotised by its tireless march, and feeling somehow a tiny step closer to our elusive goal. If I'm honest, we were unsuccessful and impressionable enough to be swayed by the Zeitgeist, and the presence of a drum machine fitted with the early nineties culture of indie music blending with electronica and sequencers and samples and loops as the herd tried to fall into the post-Roses/Mondays slip-stream. This was a time when the shadow of the second Summer of Love loomed large even over our little sun-kissed world. It was an exciting moment as there was a palpable sense that the massing tribes of young people and their unruly pursuit of good times contained that genuine note of rebellion against the establishment that had made the transgressions of fifties rock 'n' roll and punk so thrilling. It seemed briefly that dance music was destined to supplant rock, and that for rock to survive in any way it needed to adapt. Our adoption of a drum machine was a concession to this tide of fashion as we fumbled blindly in search of our own sound.

But there are often many cul-de-sacs and wrong turns on the path. Sometimes finding out where you don't want to go is as important as finding out where you *do* want to and, without wishing to sound like something printed inside a Hallmark card, it's how you overcome the mistakes and the failures that ends up defining you just as much as the successes, but ultimately it's those flaws that are so fascinating. In the same way that everyone's childhood is slightly embarrassing, so too is everyone's first stab at music. I'd love to sit here and write that we arrived fully formed, violent and dynamic, purposeful and richly eloquent, but it simply wouldn't be true. The weak, derivative, misshapen songs and the scruffy inglorious details are just as much part of the story, however, and so something of which I am strangely just as proud. Looking at other bands and their seemingly steady, untroubled ascent of the ladder makes me feel that somehow they missed something – that it's the struggle and the imperfections just as much as the finished product that gives the whole thing any heft. As the years march on it feels like the machinery that drives success is becoming more sophisticated and churns out increasingly formulaic bands via a menu of check-lists and media milestones. That type of formula was very far from being established in 1990, let alone fine-tuned, as we cast around for some sort of identity.

Probably because they were cheaper we used to attend lots of gigs at London University venues – places like University of London Union or Queen Mary College – where we would sip beer in plastic pint glasses and watch now forgotten, marginal bands like Five Thirty or That Petrol Emotion, not so much for artistic inspiration, but just to drench ourselves in the giddy world of dry ice and the squeal of feed-back, the press of bodies and the thrill of noise. One evening during the break between the support and the headliners, Bernard, Justine and I were sitting on the stairs smoking. We had reached the stage that we were searching around for a name and I can't honestly remember the story behind it, but I just remember turning to them both and saying, 'What about Suede?'

8

It's interesting how being in a band I've often found I am asked to justify and explain and intellectualise things that in retrospect seem simply instinctive. I don't remember there being an especially strong logic about our choice of name beyond the simple fact that it just sounded right. Later journalists would force me to pin some story on to the moniker, and I would try to nicely do as I was asked and blabber on about concepts of 'beauty through cruelty' and references to Elvis or Morrissey songs. But the truth is, I liked the way it sounded and I liked the way it looked and sometimes, in music and in life, that's all that really counts. So we were called Suede and armed with this new impetus and identity we marched gamely on.

The next step, of course, was to summon up the courage to take to the stage and play our songs live. I was yet to learn how crystallising and focusing this experience is in how you view your own work; that playing exactly the same song even to the most modest audience makes you view the song completely differently. When suddenly bereft of your own solipsistic perception you start to hear the song through the ears of others, its artifice peeled away and its strengths and weaknesses exposed and revealed. This we were yet to learn as we hustled for a support slot on the dreary, unforgiving, early nineties London indie circuit. We knew a boy called Andy Holland, brother of an old school friend, an art college graduate who did a bit of lighting for a band called The Prudes. He pulled some favours and used a little leverage, and we ended up being offered third on the bill at a gig they were playing at The White Horse pub on Fleet Road in Hampstead near the Royal Free Hospital. If I remember rightly the gig was in a kind of cellar below the pub. A handful of people were milling around as we gingerly stepped on stage and politely ran through our set. All I can say about the experience is that it seemed to swim by in a dream-like way. We were so nervous and out of control that some sort of autopilot instinct took over, and my memory of it is so strange and vague as to almost be repressed. I know we played 'Justice' and 'So Liberated', and possibly our newest song 'Natural Born Servant', a sort of horrible, baggy mess that we even demoed and touted hopefully and fruitlessly around a few record companies. Mat was in charge of operating the drum machine so there would probably have been sticky episodes of silence and embarrassed shuffling between the songs as he located the next programme. I'm sure it was a masterclass in ineptitude, but once the final song had been played and we had shifted our amps back off the stage, we gathered together at the bar wreathed in a rosy glow of achievement and probably relief. My most vivid memory of playing gigs during those early days was of the D-shaped space in front of the stage, a kind of no-man's land where none of the crowd would dare to venture. You almost got the sense that people didn't want to come too close to the band in case they became infected by their failure. It's funny that once a band does become successful exactly the same area is prime territory and viciously fought over and defended by hardcore fans. I also remember, way before we could even think of affording roadies, the utter bathos when after the crescendo had been reached, the final chord played and we had stormed off wrapped in what we thought was a shroud of arrogance and mystery we would have to gingerly step back on to the stage, our personas discarded, and hurry about the practicalities of shifting the gear. A year or so later when we were closing with 'To The Birds', this ridiculous disparity would be heightened even further.

We would rehearse at a place called the Premises, a shabby, old townhouse rehearsal room on Hackney Road. I think it's still there. It was draughty and scruffy and naturally noisy but kind of cosy. There was sweet tea and paraffin heaters, and the smell of stale smoke and sweat and the cigarette butts of a thousand unsigned bands. We would thrash away until late in the evening as east London muttered and screeched a couple of floors below. At some point, after inheriting a little money from my lovely old Uncle Harry, I had bought a beautiful Rickenbacker six-string electric which Justine would faithfully strum as Bernard leapt around the frets of his Epiphone and the drum machine pattered on. Mat would rumble away on his old Fender bass, and sometimes during fag breaks would jokingly conduct mock interviews or challenge me into showing him how I intended to move on stage. Mat is without doubt one of the cleverest and sharpest people you are ever likely to meet. He has the ability to make amusing off-the-cuff quips that most people would take weeks to come up with. Today, he has aged into a kind and happy man, and his acerbic bone-dry wit is still always funny, but when he was younger this ruthless mockery could sometimes feel probing and teasing. Fortunately, having spent so much time together I knew how to bat him off, and would just mumble something inaudible in my nasal estuary drawl and wander off to make tea. From quite early on, though, once the existing hierarchy had been deconstructed, Bernard would be leading the proceedings, constantly turning up with new pieces to rehearse on to which I would try to weld lyrics and melodies. Even in those very early days when we were still inept and unloved, his industry was inspiring. It was one of the many things that over the years I really admired about him: that relentless, restless zeal, that mission to create. Slowly, I think Bernard began to feel more comfortable with us. Our close dynamic must have felt intimidating at first and, of course, he was from a very different background to Justine, but then again we all were. He was always a step apart from us, though, and I got the sense that rather than there being an immediate empathy, he began to trust us as he learned to blend. I suppose the seeds of discord were sown within us many years before they actually ended up growing and tearing us apart, but for the moment we learned to repress any slight uneasiness as we gamely pressed on and papered over our differences. Whereas the rest of us would blather on constantly about anything and everything, Bernard was more introspective and intense. They say that the quietest people have the loudest minds, and I got the impression that he internalised things and expressed them through the music he was writing rather than through any conversations that I had with him at the time. But who really knows? We were only just beginning to understand each other and our period of real bonding was still a year or so away.

We managed to convince another small-time

promoter to put us on – a guy called Chris who ran
the Cube Club, an indie venue in a decent-sized room
with a high stage at the back of the Bull and Gate on
Kentish Town Road, just down from the far more
prestigious Town and Country Club where proper
bands with fans and actual record deals played. All
I remember from that night was the feeling of complete horror as the drum machine decided to break
down a couple of times, and with a deathly finality
stop mid-song. We froze like four frightened rabbits,
confused and panicked, the foundations wrenched
from under us as Mat scrambled for the controls in
an ecstasy of fumbling, and I probably tried in vain to
mumble something witty or charismatic to cover the
embarrassed shuffling silence and muffled sniggers.
Incredibly, in spite of this comedy of errors, Chris
managed to see something in us and booked us for
another show. He was the first person outside our
little circle to ever have faith in us and I don't think
I've ever really thanked him for that.

The next gig was a support slot with Clare Grogan
from Altered Images as the headliner. It's a mark of
our lowly position on the slippery ladder of success
that such an opportunity seemed glamorous to us; like

we were somehow within tantalising touching distance of fame, no matter how minor or how vicarious.
It's ironic that once we had eventually got somewhere
our popular image for many was as members of
some closed circle of the urbane metropolitan elite:
the cool and connected Londoners who saw success
as their birthright, rubbing shoulders with the great
and the good. Nothing could have been further from
the truth as we timidly climbed on to the stage at
the Bull and Gate and unconvincingly ran through
our set to a smattering of vaguely distracted Altered
Images fans. The truth is that all of us felt utterly
excluded by the media and its power brokers because
we were. We were like grubby-cheeked urchins with
our faces pressed up against the window of a sweet
shop: unlikely, unconnected and adrift. Apart from
Justine who had looked privilege in the face, I think
the rest of us had grown up with the notion that success was something that happened to other people.
None of us knew anyone who had ever penetrated
the inner circles of the media's hushed and moneyed
playgrounds; our parents were taxi drivers and factory
workers and unskilled labourers who were only likely
to have met a celebrity or journalist or an A&R man

if they had given them a lift home in their cab. It was this distance that's always given me the feeling that, even when successful, the band were somehow always outsiders. Years later, when we appeared on the Brits, I remember the Green Room being full of puffed-up, self-important celebrities like Cher and Peter Gabriel mincing around in their ridiculous costumes while we just smoked and laughed with the make-up girls at the utter naffness of it all. I've always cherished that sense of outsiderdom to be honest – that healthy disrespect – and always believed that the voices that come from the margins have a truthfulness and that as an artist as soon as you are fully accepted and part of an elite you are somehow neutered.

So our free time began to be filled by the soul-crushing experience of trying to enter the sweet shop. Bernard and I would spend whole afternoons licking stamps and sending out demo tapes in yellow Jiffy bags and being put on hold by record companies and low-level promoters and venue owners who were always 'away from their desks'. Calls were not taken and doors were shut in our faces. So we thought we'd use Justine's obvious charms as bait in our desperate, depressing crusade. A couple of times she went into places like East West or Chrysalis Records dressed in a leather skirt to try to press one of our cassettes into the hands of someone who might make a difference. It sounds terrible now, but it was nothing sordid – we all just thought with her looks and her allure she would probably have more chance of getting noticed than us skinny, wan-looking boys. But the record companies never called us back, and thank god they didn't – we still desperately needed to improve.

After hustling and jostling and persevering, however, we managed to get our song 'Wonderful, Sometimes' played on Gary Crowley's *Demo Clash* one Sunday afternoon on GLR. It was a part of the show where Gary would play two unsigned bands' tracks back to back, the public would vote for the best and the winner would go through to the following week's contest. Of course, in reality all this indicated was how many friends each band could muster up to bother to phone in, and as we knew quite a few people we ended up winning a couple of times. The minor ripple of attention from this provoked a *Melody Maker* journalist to come to the Bull and Gate to review the gig but it was way too early for us, and the ensuing vicious, waspish critique stung horribly. I think we were likened to children's TV presenters, and if you ever see any early photos from those shows the description isn't unjustified. Dressed hilariously in awful, stripy, post-Madchester, Day-Glo T-shirts and loose jeans we must have thought were fashionable, we had all the charisma and presence of toilet-roll holders. It was our first bitter slap of harsh public censure but I guess it became part of the tapestry of events that ended up making us improve. And god knows we needed to. Even though in the early nineties the word 'career' was certainly never bandied about when talking about music, there was still a strong sense that our struggle was much more than some vague whim. In the pre-digital age it seemed perfectly feasible to expect that putting food on the table and making interesting, marginal music weren't mutually exclusive. Nowadays I know of even relatively successful, creative and inspiring alternative bands – seasoned, professional and hard-working outfits – whose members need to supplement their incomes with part-time jobs. The implications for the future of creativity in music are bleak indeed.

So we soldiered clumsily on for a few months, playing along to the drum machine's capricious, clockwork tyranny at a string of semi-deserted, depressing gigs in the back rooms of pubs and in now closed-down, low-level venues, but it slowly began to dawn on us that if we wanted the songs to breathe in any way, if we wanted them to grow and evolve and provoke a response that wasn't just muttering and silence and a smattering of dutiful applause, then we needed to find a real drummer.

Somehow or other we got in contact with a boy called Justin Welch. He turned up at the Premises one evening with his drums in the back of his Mini, a shocking little rocker with shoulder-length, ash-blond hair, a thick Midlands accent and a ring through his nose. I've always really liked Justin and we still hang out with him to this day. He's always lovely and great fun to have around, but when he was young he had this tireless, whirlwind energy that left behind a trail of chaos. We ran through some songs with him, and he smashed and crashed and rolled along like a cross between Keith Moon and Animal from *The Muppets*. But it sounded great: breathing with life and space, and free at last from the drum machine's skittish, rigid punch. He was the sort of guy who played with loads of bands, however, and I'm not sure if our polite, still slightly sexless songs really spoke to him. We vaguely decided to meet up again, but I sensed that he was prevaricating. Afterwards we all decided to go for a drink, and I ended up squashed into his Mini, pressed up against the kit. He drove like he played the drums, and as we raced along Hackney Road he took a corner too fast, lost control and span the car. We ended up skidding around in a perfect circle like we were stunt men in a cop-show car chase. When we finally screeched to a halt, the first thing we saw in front of us was a police van and a row of three frowning, angry cops, who had witnessed the whole episode, staring back at us through the windscreen. Justin spent the next couple of hours at the police station, and the rest of us went home thirsty.

Now I really can't be bothered to get the order of events right here because that isn't the point of this book, but at some juncture a guy Mat and I knew from Haywards Heath Sixth Form College appeared on the scene. He obviously had a bit of money and wanted to dabble in the music business a bit by starting a record label, so he said he'd pay for us to record a couple of things. Even though it probably technically was, it didn't *feel* like a proper record deal. It was much too low key and low end to have any of that sense of glamour or privilege. For one thing his homemade 'label' had no history or identity or roster: just three anonymous-sounding letters and a modest promise. I don't remember actually signing anything, and I certainly don't remember it feeling pivotal or particularly exciting, but it did mean that we got to spend a bit of time in a proper studio – some place he'd found for us down in Sussex, ironically not a million miles from Haywards Heath. For anyone who grows up on a diet of rock biographies and rainy afternoons scouring the *NME*, the iconography of recording studios assumes a thrillingly familiar lustre, so much of our time there amongst the maze of control rooms and baffled sound booths was spent wandering around like wide-eyed children who have found the keys to a secret garden, running our fingers along the faders and keyboards, lost in our own private rock fantasies. The business of actually recording something seemed somehow secondary but eventually we gathered our composure and took our first faltering steps to properly committing our ideas. Often the song that a band is most excited about is the latest one that's been written. At that time ours was called 'Be My God' – a pulsing, hypnotic, almost celestial groove that started with Bernard's guitar washing and growing through a volume pedal, but which was let down by my weak singing and nothing lyrics. We stumbled on with the process, however, enjoying its novel thrill, and after a couple of days within the enclave of rec rooms and mixing desks we had finished the track and drove back up the M23 to London with the tapes, wired and breathless with plans and possibility.

Our links with him were fairly casual, so in that insouciant, bondless way that young people often have, Justin drifted off to play for Spitfire or one of his many other bands sometime after we returned and we were forced to search for a new drummer and so decided to place another music press advert. I can't remember the exact wording but I know we namechecked The Smiths as an influence. One of the few people who answered was a Mancunian called Mike. What we didn't know until he marched into the rehearsal room at the Premises was that it was Mike Joyce. We were all slightly in awe, but Mike was a real gentleman. He politely listened to our average songs and jammed along with us and offered advice, but never monologued or lectured or played the seasoned pro. Over the next few weeks he would take us under his wing and in his kind, avuncular way try to nurture and encourage us. I'd like to think he must have seen some potential, but maybe he just felt sorry for us or liked hanging out. Anyway, Bernard and I travelled up on the train to Manchester one time to stay with him and his wife. We jammed in his cellar and wrote a funny song there called 'We Believe In Showbiz' and drank tea and chatted and smoked into the night. He told us some old war stories and in the morning he dropped us off at Piccadilly Station and we went back to London feeling cared for and somehow less excluded. A few weeks later we booked some time at Battery Studios in London to record another new song on which Mike was to play drums: 'Art', appropriately a driving, powerful beast with a guitar part that was reminiscent of the rockier moments of *Meat Is Murder*. Sadly, my vocal line again let it down and the song struggled to come across as anything other than bluster and empty fury. I simply hadn't yet learned how to deliver melody properly; the lyrics were too crammed and hurried, and I was trying to say too much but ended up saying nothing. Still, things would change and we were beginning to learn the art of patience.

The promised release of the tracks never

materialised – the 'record company' obviously realising that it didn't actually have much to hang anything
on. Unfortunately, our mistake in committing too
early would come back to haunt us once we had
achieved success, as we had to buy back the recordings
to prevent an embarrassing release of substandard
material at a time when every single moment of what
we were doing was being microscopically scrutinised.
Our time with Mike ended on very good terms, however, both parties realising that there would be an
unfair disparity and imbalance if he actually joined
the band, so we stayed friends and he drifted off to
play with PIL, and we began looking for yet another
drummer. I still see Mike from time to time and am
always cheered by the fact that his warmth and passion never seem to burn less brightly.

During his time at Queen Mary College Bernard
had met a chap called Nadir who began to manage us.
He was part of a team of low-level university events
managers that included a person who worked at the
ULU ticket office called Ricky. He introduced us to
a drummer who he worked with there and we set up
an audition with him at the Premises. His name was
Simon Gilbert. I remember Simon walking in and

being shy and polite and extremely charming, and to this day even though he seems less shy and has over the years revealed depths of warmth and kindness, my perception of him hasn't changed much. He was dressed in his ubiquitous DMs, tight trousers and spiked-up, bottle-blond hair, and looked a bit like a missing member of The Clash – not that different from how he looks today really. We played through a couple of numbers and it was clear quite early on that he was the missing element. I've always loved Simon's style of drumming: never too fussy, always primal and powerful and obviously hugely influenced by Paul Cook and Budgie and Topper Headon and all the rough, angry music I first fell in love with. Simon's input was such a key, often overlooked, factor in the kind of band we went on to be. I think he made us veer away from any ill-advised excursions into 'groove', and teased out all of the punk and post-punk elements that were lying dormant in the band. The tribal tom pattern of 'The Drowners', the frenetic chaos of songs like 'Moving' and 'Dolly', and the vicious edge of our early music would have evolved very differently in the hands of another drummer. The rest of us were so sure that he fitted in that we didn't actually bother telling Simon himself, and even after weeks of increasingly exciting rehearsals, I remember him timidly calling me up one day and politely asking whether he'd passed the audition, something for which sometimes we still affectionately pull his leg.

The band finally complete, we set about furiously writing and rehearsing. With Simon in place we started to develop a harder edge and wrote nastier, punkier songs like 'Going Blonde' and 'Painted People', and at last I was beginning to come up with parts that don't now embarrass me. 'Going Blonde' was a kind of frenetic, stream-of-consciousness rant, inspired a little by the scattered, crammed metre of 'Subterranean Homesick Blues' and featuring a fictional character called Terry that Justine and I had invented. He inhabited a slightly idealised, working-class, fantasy world of pool halls and cheap lager and fake-diamond ear studs, and his character was very much inspired by Martin Amis's *London Fields*, a book with which I became a little obsessed way back in 1990. Justine always loved the lyrics, and Elastica would later cover it and retitle it 'See That Animal' (as it started off with me shouting 'See that animal/

Get some heavy metal!'). 'Painted People', a sardonic, high-life, mocking tirade was one of the oldest songs that eventually saw the light of day and we sometimes still play it; its short, unpleasant, hectoring diatribe always provides a neat rush of adrenalised anger. And as Simon provided the jigsaw's missing piece so Mat started to evolve in parallel, writing ever more ambitious basslines that meshed with the thump of the live drums and added another layer of identity to the music; never happy to simply occupy a frequency or plod along, but often complex and rich with melody. Mat had previously always been much more conceptual about music. I think he'd be the first to agree that he was never a 'musician's musician' and never really wanted to be; his strengths, hugely important to the band as they were, lay more in his vision and his taste. He was always the one who had the most finely developed consciousness about the kind of band that we were and the kind of band that we wanted to be, and to this day his is still such a vital voice. Without him, songs with the self-awareness of something like 'Trash' might never have come about, and certainly my own sense of a band having a 'world' and a specific landscape that it operated within would have lain underdeveloped. Simon's presence, however, unlocked something very musical in him and he started coming up with fantastic parts: 'He's Dead', 'Pantomime Horse', 'To The Birds' and later stuff like 'She's Not Dead' and 'The Wild Ones' had beautiful, moving basslines in their own right and Mat's playing was utterly essential to the sound and feel of those early songs.

Simon's first gig with us was probably at the Rock Garden. I think it might have been one of those 'pay-to-play' venues where desperate young bands were exploited into stumping up cash for their own performances in order to provide themselves with a thin patina of exposure. I don't remember a great deal about the show itself. I'm assuming we were received with the same general indifferent shrug by the audience, but it felt to us that we were now at last heading somewhere. Somewhere of our own.

Incidentally, the Ricky who worked with Simon at ULU was Ricky Gervais. You'll be sorry to hear I didn't have a huge amount to do with him at the time. Simon is actually the best source for those old war stories. I've probably met him more times since we've both achieved success than beforehand, and he has always been generous and charming to a fault, and naturally very droll, often remarking that he was pleased for me that I 'never got fat'. The only time our paths really crossed in the dark ages of the early nineties was when we supported his band – Son Of Bleeper – at some scantily attended university do. I hope he wouldn't think it unfair of me to say that looking back he came across as a less funny version of David Brent with some truly wince-inducing songs. One in particular contained lyrics that stuck in my head for years. It was something along the lines of 'What Johnny wants to do is make his guitar sing the blues' sung in this sort of throaty, neo-American, blue-collar, bar-room voice. I think Ricky's genius moment came when he realised that the richest source of comedy available to him was actually himself.

9

At some point during early 1991 while all this was happening, Justine had met someone else. The magic and the thrill had become tarnished by the grind of familiarity and routine and the frustrations of failure. We were young and without the ties of family, and I suppose she had glimpsed what she thought was a better life for herself. Possibly, like my father before me, I had drifted into a comfortable indolence; my ridiculous idealisation of the romance of idling and my rejection of ambition must have made life with me become slightly dull. If people want to cackle and crow and hear that I was crushed then, yes, I willingly concede that I was. The only thing that was really holding me together after the death of my mum was the glue of our relationship, and to have that suddenly wrenched away from me exposed the raw wound of bereavement still further, and left me toppling and spinning with the push and the stab of it all. It might seem odd to people that a young man in his early twenties could allow himself to become so damaged by something as predictable as a lovers' break-up. I wonder myself sometimes. I suppose I was still an emotionally frail person, but fiercely loyal to those I considered worthy of my loyalty. In times of betrayal these fictions crumble like sandcastles, and again like my father before me I am left lying broken on the floor clutching desperately at the thin air of my fantasies. I was young and I was in love for the first time, and when that dizzying high is over it's a long, long way down. The break-up was nasty, horrible even, full of endless fraught phone calls and long tearful evenings that melted into lonely coal black mornings as I floundered and clung. I should have just calmly walked away but our lives had become so entwined it seemed impossible. So we struggled along messily for a while, bound together in a bitter cloud of recrimination and frustration and betrayal, all of the joy and harmony of our former life horribly inverted, until one evening I couldn't take it any more, collected my things, called a minicab and left, leaving behind a few shirts and some old Popscene annuals I'd picked up in a junk shop.

I think for vast swathes of a young man's life he feels a bit like George Bone from Patrick Hamilton's *Hangover Square*: excluded and rejected, forever on the fringe of acceptance, the soft, gossamer world of the feminine cruelly denied him, its pleasures dangling tantalisingly out of reach. It was back to this cold, hard, friendless landscape I felt I had returned as I wrestled with my ignominious demotion and trudged back on to the familiar, dog shit-strewn pavements of my single life. If I were forced to use clinical language, I would describe myself at my core as a co-dependant person; a romantic who seeks completion through others and through fantasy, strangely never quite whole just as myself. It's possible that this flaw in me, this imbalance, is the motor which generally drives my need to constantly write songs; fulfilling the old cliché about seeking to create perfection in art when it doesn't exist in life. Certainly, these massive shifts in my life started to be subtly expressed in the person I was becoming, and once the pain had faded I eventually assimilated the loss in the form of an overt femininity that I explored as a style during those first early flushes of success. People would interpret it as some sort of fake gay thing or a nod to seventies glam, or something similarly dreary, but looking back I'm convinced I was trying to replace the feminine absence in my life with an ersatz one of my own making. It sounds bizarre and deluded, and naturally it came across as gaudy and more than faintly ridiculous, but at its heart, as was the case with so many things to do with the Suede sensibility, it was an expression of grief. Together I had felt complete, but faced with that chasm of emptiness that death and loss deliver I felt utterly imbalanced and in need of redressing that. Looking at it now, it sounds weak and mawkish and faintly pathetic. I'm not proud of the way I dealt with this, but it was a confusing time and I was still emotionally very raw, and in many ways very much unformed as a person. This idea of replacing people with gestures and things fed into some of those early songs. Something like 'Dolly' was very much about projecting emotions on to an object, in this case a mannequin, partly inspired by the famous, twisted story of Phil Spector insisting his wife drive around with a dummy resembling him. Many years later the film *Lars and the Real Girl* dealt with this subject so brilliantly and wittily, and its provenance in pop music is probably that early Roxy Music song, but at the time I wasn't consciously aware of it despite what people might assume.

I moved into a crumbling, stucco-fronted, first-floor flat in Moorhouse Road in the little enclave between Notting Hill and Bayswater that the estate agents now call Artesian Village, a part of London I would stay in for the next twenty-five years. Now the area is plush and well-heeled, lined with the whispered hush of money and privilege. In the early nineties, many years before Hugh Grant and Julia Roberts would turn its fortunes, the rows of faded, once prosperous Victorian terraces were full of deserted, boarded-up houses that sat dark and empty like missing teeth, and instead of boutiques Westbourne Grove was full of charity shops like Sue Ryder and Cancer Research, and the only coffee you could buy was instant. My old friend Alan Fisher had become bored with life in Brighton, and as the little flat had enough space for two beds he moved in and paid half the paltry rent. Despite its cheap metal sink and peeling walls I loved that flat and went about decorating it with bric-à-brac that I picked up at the scruffy end of Portobello Market up by Goldborne Road. I covered the place in images and ephemera: random ironic pictures of seventies pop stars and old album sleeves, and I hung antique glass beads from above the doorway lintels and put a surreal, gimpy-looking, black-plastic donkey on the balcony. We found most of our furniture on the street as people used to dump their stuff down by the bins at the church on the corner and Alan had a terrapin which lived in the bath. The flat was bathed in the warm glow of red light bulbs and there were odd, cheap *objets* and mounds of mildewy, second-hand books and piles of old albums everywhere. We found a stray black cat and called him Meisk. He came complete with fleas that so infested the place that if you put your hand on the floor-boards it would slowly turn black with their massing army of tiny bodies. A couple of years later while I was on tour in America he would be lost. I called Alan from some diner in Wisconsin one day to ask him how everything was only to be told that things were fine except that the cat had disappeared for a couple of days and had eventually come back home 'a bit fluffier'. I frowned but thought nothing of it until I eventually returned to London, unwashed and tour weary, to find a completely different cat sitting on the bed. Alan had panicked and replaced Meisk with the first cat he had seen on the street that looked vaguely similar. I eventually found out where he had been kidnapped from and returned him, but Meisk had slipped away, his tiny sleek, black body and mask of intense indifference lost for ever to the friendless London streets.

Alan and I became obsessed with early Mike Leigh films and things like Orton's *Entertaining Mr Sloane* and especially Nic Roeg's *Performance*, which was shot in Powis Square down the road, watching it on a loop and learning all the dialogue, enjoying the parallels with the film's odd, marginal characters living in another strange, decaying house in Notting Hill. In the flat upstairs lived an artist, the pre-success Anish Kapoor, and the flat above him was occupied by a wiry gay skinhead called Kevin; hard as nails, but sweet and kind and fiercely loyal to his friends. He and his boyfriend both died of AIDS later in the decade and I wrote the lyrics to 'The Living Dead' about them, trying to tease out some poetry from the struggle of their narcotic pact.

I knew Alan from years earlier and had always loved his fidgety, mischievous charm and his spirit of almost ruthless hedonism. We became extremely close as we fumbled around the edges of west London together dressed in fake fur coats and unwashed trousers. A year or so later he would inspire me to write the lyrics to both 'High Rising' and 'The Big Time' and would play a huge role within my idealised sketches of the London demi-monde on half the songs from *Coming Up*. In different ways 'The Big Time' and 'High Rising' were both intended as sad farewells to him. The former was a slightly ruthless dissection of the schisms created by success and ambition, but 'High Rising' was meant to be more tender; a song born of the countless mornings when I would have to rise early and catch planes, and as I took off from Heathrow and soared over London I would look down from my window seat and imagine him waking and waving up at me from the mess and chaos of our little flat. *Withnail and I* was inevitably a touchstone for us, and the moving and beautiful final scene in Regent's Park Zoo was an inspiration point for both of these songs. The endless smoky nights sat around glass-topped tables together in the mid-nineties, and the parade of bizarre and unusual friends we began to acquire would directly inform the lyrics to 'Beautiful Ones' as I tried to capture the madness and the scatty, unhinged fun of those days. The endless mornings-after and their sense of isolated camaraderie and refusal to engage became the bedrock of songs like 'Lazy' as we both flopped and floundered in the debris of the night before. To quote Ariel Levy: 'We had brutal hangovers – but we had them together'. We started smoking sweet clove cigarettes called Caravan. They were dark brown and crackled as they burned, filling the flat with their delicious, cloying smell. We would crave them and trek at all hours down to the only outlet that sold them, a little tobacconist's just off the Tottenham Court Road; yet another regular stop for me as I shuttled back and forth along the Central Line. Alan worked in a chip-shop down in Surrey and would lever himself out of bed at around midday, struggle down to Victoria and then on to a train, and spend most of the day and night huddled over an industrial deep-fat fryer returning to the flat around midnight stinking of fried cod. After he'd covered himself in aftershave we would go out, either traipsing round All Saints Road trying to score pot or sometimes to a bizarre late-night Austrian cellar bar called The Tiroler Hut on Westbourne Grove that served cheese fondues and Jägermeister until two in the morning. Alan had worked hard and made a bit of money so he bought himself an old gun-metal-grey nineteen sixties vintage Daimler and we would rattle around in it feeling like the Krays. Unfortunately, he was an unbelievably bad driver. He would never tell me whether he had actually passed his test or was just using his twin brother's licence. Anyway, stepping into a car with Alan could be perilous. At one point he managed to write off three cars in three weeks before he finally gave up and we started taking the tube everywhere again. Motorway journeys with him could be terrifying. I remember sitting in the passenger's seat one chilly misty morning, both of us a little worse for wear after having played a student ball at Cambridge. Juggernauts thundered and sprayed past us sounding their horns like klaxons as we weaved and doddered near the hard shoulder; Alan shaking and chattering and gurning as he chain-smoked endless Caravan cigarettes, and I desperately tried to keep him focused and us both alive. A sucker for punishment and obviously possessing a short memory, when I'd made some money in the late nineties I bought a nice car and as I had no licence needed a driver so I gave Alan the job. I think he lasted a day before I hired a professional.

There was always a bizarre menagerie of characters hanging around the flat who would tag along or who we would invite back: Antipodean drifters or Swedish twentysomething nannies or sometimes the slightly damaged, fragile occupants of the social housing flats at the end of the road. We would sit around chatting and smoking, listening to 'The Bewlay Brothers' late into the night, and sometimes I'd get out my old Aria Elecord and make them sit through renditions of 'That's Entertainment' or 'A Day In The Life'. Our friend Tamzin Drew, who had coincidentally also gone to Oathall, would often waft by and would sit around the flat like a quiet Victorian ghost talking to the cat or sketching us for one of her beautiful, surreal illustrations. Or our friend Laurie, a sweet hippy who had possibly taken far too much acid in his life, would drop by shoeless and wild-eyed and brimming with stories and extraordinary theories. It was all still fairly soft and innocent; the sweet, light, unhinged madness helping to numb the twin pains of separation and bereavement until everyone went home and the bleak nights would close in around me again.

The flat in Moorhouse Road became in a way a key element in the formation of the debut album. Everything was broken and grimy and second-hand but magical and charming, and slowly this fascinating duality of faded elegance and harsh, stark poverty began to seep into what I was writing about and the vision that was forming for the band. It became a sort of microcosm of our outer world, a tatty, wonderful stage on which many of the sticky, gaudy dramas that inspired those early songs were played out. All the bizarre drunken trysts and unlikely moments, the still, dead-eyed hours watching the slow hands of the clock: they all fed into the world I was writing about and became just as important as any band or album that the press would later latch on to. It's funny how these huge personal influences almost always escape mention by the media, albeit understandably so, as they are outside its sphere of reference. But it's important to recognise how friends or lovers or towns or streets or a flat I once lived in have been just as influential to my songs as whole movements in rock.

While Alan was at work frying chips I began to spend more and more time with Bernard and we became close. I've never really liked being with big gangs of people – I find it confusing and intimidating and diminishing, and I'm somehow unable to be myself – but faced with one person I open up and relax. I think both Bernard and I are actually the kind of people who find it easier to communicate like this, so away from the spotlight of the band's social hierarchies and now that I was single there was more space and we became freer and easier together. Behind the prickly mask he sometimes wore there was revealed a sweet, thoughtful boy who kindly helped me glue together the pieces of my fractured world. To be honest, I find it hard to talk about my and Bernard's 'relationship'. It became such an irritating and intrusive issue to us years later when we re-formed with The Tears, and seemed to dominate any interview with its looming, distracting presence, so that I don't feel like I can add anything to the mountain of contradiction and misinformation. While we just wanted to talk about the songs we had written and the album that we were proud of, everyone else was just obsessed with the soap opera of our personal history, like some

sort of dull, gossipy, indie *Hello!*, powder-puff cover
story. As with any two people forced together into the
crucible of work and success, there are tensions and
frustrations, but there needs to be love and respect
and real warmth too. In fact, there's a good argument
that friction in a decent writing team is essential for
it to work; that the push and pull and the needling
and the goading and the inherent sense of challenge
are an essential part of its chemistry, and that each of
you needs to accept that as part of the pact and learn
to deal with it. Even now, nearly thirty years later,
and as a relatively successful writer with decades of
experience, I still find the process of making albums
an ordeal that stretches the boundaries of the interper-
sonal relationships between me and the people with
whom I make them. You can find yourself projecting
frustrations on to others or childishly blaming them
for failures and inertia, until you gently tap yourself
on the shoulder and remind yourself that failure and
inertia are points on the path, and that the challenge
is always, always actually a challenge within yourself.
My relationship with Bernard wasn't any different
in that respect – it's just that the media spotlight
on us became so intense at one point that it became

magnified, and the schisms became mutated and distorted in its unforgiving glare. We were just too young to realise that the frictions weren't 'personal' at all, but merely a by-product of the creative process that we were too naive to know how to deal with. Sadly, this would eventually lead to implosion and collapse as the media worried the wounds in that blithe and unaccountable way that they do, but I only have sunny, fond memories of our time together during the early years. Yes, there were the usual silences and sulks that litter any creative path, but at this point, before the distorting prisms of success and money coloured us for ever, I'd like to think that we were friends. Obviously, we have always been quite different people, but maybe not quite as different as people might think. In my experience, if there is any rumour of drama between members of a band, those outside the inner circle will automatically project what they think they know about these frictions on to the meanings of the songs and interpret the words through that lens. Countless times I've read that this song or that song is 'about' Bernard because it 'might' contain an element that 'might' relate to the dynamics of our relationship, when in fact the song almost always has a completely different, much more veiled origin. I saw the same sort of thing happening in the next decade with The Libertines when everything you read about them fed into the turbulent romance of their interlocking personalities, and I'm sure, as was the case with us, most of it was complete fiction. But I totally understand how important the back story is for many people; that the intrigue and the rumour imbues the music with substance and heft, and clothes it in a tantalising veil. It's just important to remember that it's all subjective and that there are no absolute truths, even for the writer.

We were constantly shuttling back and forth on the Central Line to Bernard's place in Leyton, or he'd come over to Notting Hill and we would listen to music and plot and plan, and it would all feed into the songs we had begun to write. At the time, when he was still terminally unfashionable, I was having an early Bowie rediscovery period and became obsessed with the lyrics to 'Quicksand', especially his mention of 'the power' which started to be something that I interpreted as the elusive key to song-writing, and I remember sitting on the floor in front of the three-bar fire in Bernard's flat one chilly afternoon blathering on about it. I'm not sure if Bernard was as well versed in Bowie's *oeuvre* as I was but he fell in love with it, and it became the music, and later the strait jacket, that along with The Smiths we would use to reference and initially define ourselves.

It was, of course, a complex tapestry of events but possibly the single most potent engine for change in me, apart from the growing chemistry of the band and our development as writers, was my becoming single. Had I remained within my soft, jolly little bubble it's likely that Suede would never have happened, certainly not in any meaningful way. As a young man I had a tendency towards a state of cosy lassitude, and I needed to experience those seismic changes to overcome that and to express the sense of loss and rage that I was feeling and to step up and start to match the quality of what Bernard had been doing for a while. I've always performed best as an artist when faced with adversity; when forced to kick against something or overcome a hurdle. Whenever I've found things too easy I've tended to switch off and produce anodyne work. Boringly, I am probably circumscribed within the clichéd parameters of the 'tortured artist' archetype; needing to seek out tensions and frictions as a catalyst to create. The body blows of bereavement and lost love created the perfect environment in me, and like bacteria in a Petri dish it all began to grow into something fascinating. The truth was that before that event my writing had yet to acquire any form or tone, or real personality. I had vague sensibilities towards documenting a kind of romanticised 'beautiful loser' sort of lifestyle – weak songs like 'She's A Layabout' and 'Natural Born Servant' idealised dole life and inaction and afternoons wasted sat watching Australian soap operas – but without the poetry or skill or wit to yet paint it as anything other than stereotype. Looking back, I think I was trying to infuse my family's humble origins with some sense of grace and dignity. I always felt sad that my parents and their parents before them had lived and died within the four grey walls of poverty, and I was desperate to give meaning to our shabby world of second-hand clothes and free school meals and meaningless dead-end jobs. It was born from a kind of inverted snobbery, an elitism probably inherited from my father whereby I saw the social parameters into which I was born as something to be celebrated. Well, what other choice did I have? It seemed unlikely that I would escape them anytime soon. Unfortunately, the writing just came across as vague and slightly bitter, and without any proper command of melody it lacked any real presence or thrust. Tempered with the agonies of loss and the chaos of displacement, however, all these notions suddenly began to crystallise into something pertinent, and became imbued with a passion and a sense of drama. Suddenly, wonderfully, the songs started to appear. Another giant leap for us was also, for want of a better phrase, the emergence of sex in our writing. I don't necessarily mean titillating, salacious references in the lyrics, I mean something at the core of the music: the pounding rhythms, the primal guitar parts and in my increasingly unruly delivery as a singer. When I listen to the demos of those early songs like 'Natural Born Servant' or 'So Liberated', the most accurate way I can describe them is 'sexless'. It sounds like music made by virgins – there's nothing carnal or troubling about it, there's no passion and no guts and it all feels self-consciously wordy and limp. The moment that Bernard and I started to dig deep inside ourselves and tap into those primal urges like anger and hatred and lust was the moment that we really grew as writers. One day I went over to Bernard's in Leyton, and he ushered me into his flat and excitedly played me a demo. It started with a pounding, tribal, drum-machine pattern followed by slabs of stabbing, almost glammy guitar. We looked at each other and I think we both knew something had changed. I hurried home with the cassette and spent all day and all night writing, and by the morning we had 'The Drowners': the song that was, in a way, destined to change all of our lives. I remember sitting outside on the balcony in Moorhouse Road smoking and hammering away on my old, portable typewriter and when Alan came back, pouncing on him in a frenzy of excitement and thrusting the lyrics proudly in his face, knowing that we were on to something special. 'The Drowners' was never actually 'about' the split, whatever that means, but 'Pantomime Horse' and 'To The Birds' and 'He's Dead' and 'Moving' and a host of others were torn from those lonely coal black mornings, born from those pools of reflection and regret. And looking back it was all so, so worth it as the wisdom of Michael J. Fox's famous quote about pain being temporary slowly revealed itself. These weren't weak, tuneless songs about nothing; they were towering and passionate, and brimming with grace and drama and violence. Suddenly it was all beginning to make sense; the failure and the bitter gnawing jealousy was pouring itself into the songs that I was writing and feeding them with narrative and purpose. It felt like at last we had found 'the power'.

'The Drowners' was deliberately oblique but toying with some of the themes of ambiguity I was developing and set within a very familiar world of suffocating, failing relationships. It was based loosely around my time spent with a Canadian girl I had met called Laura. She lived in a squat just opposite Victoria Park in Hackney in a huge crumbling house that today is probably worth millions but in the early nineties smelled of cat food and patchouli, and was infested by tribes of speeding, Doc Marten-booted Goth girls in stripy tights and shambling crusties with nose-rings. She was fascinating, if sometimes saturnine, company and I enjoyed the endless hours in her mysterious, occasionally witchy presence; her lacy, shadowy world of tarot cards and incense and Hole records. The 'taking me over' refrain of the song was the first time I ever really mastered the power of the vocal 'hook'; that childishly simple sounding *mot juste* that can be so elusive but so worth the chase.

This was London in the early nineties, hugely different from the popular 'Cool Britannia' revisionist myth that media hindsight has over-simplistically projected on to that whole decade. It's a popular theory that decades only 'get going' halfway through and the nineties was no exception. It felt like the first few years at least were a hangover of the eighties: John Major's irrelevant, dreary, Tory world of unemployment and cut-price lager and crap boy bands. The sparkle and promise of the eighties had long passed – the macabre 'champagne and skyscrapers' fantasy twisted into a bleak no-man's land of flimsy phone boxes and ugly logos and desperate men in cheap suits. Nothing seemed to work properly and everywhere was painted in the same landlord magnolia. Even the more salubrious parts of London looked tired and worn and dusted with a fine patina of grime, and the rest of the capital felt like a car park or a waiting room. And culturally the outlook was just as barren; the generation-defining bands were temporarily extinct creating a vacuum into which was sucked a landfill of faceless, anodyne dance music and charisma-less pop. Even the alternative scene had run out of ideas as the weekly music press scrabbled around for some sort of purchase after the baggy and shoegazing movements had spluttered out and aborted in such a spectacularly meaningless manner. This was the world that I was both reacting against and documenting. There was always a strange dance between those two poles, and any 'glamour' that our songs contained was intended to be an escapist one, certainly not some dull, ironic nineteen seventies homage, but positioned firmly within the place from which their inhabitants were escaping: the rented rooms, the littered pavements and the dull throb of last night's hangover.

The song 'He's Dead' especially reminds me of those desperate, hungry years. Whereas virtually everything else came about in the same way, with me writing top lines to Bernard's incipient musical ideas, this song was unusually something that I initiated, sliding a sort of F sharp-shaped chord up and down the frets but leaving the top E and B strings open and droning. It was simple but effective, and suggested something reflective and murky, so I wrote a lyric about depression set within a hostile, friendless world of roundabouts and squats. After leaving college I'd just started signing on and every week would take the tube to Edgware Road and trudge down to the Lisson Grove dole office, and stand in a queue in my second-hand clothes and be lectured and harangued by officials in exchange for a few quid a week. 'He's Dead' was very much set within that dreary landscape: the drizzle, the traffic islands, the feeling of the wet pavement against my socks. The music was over-simplistic until Bernard wrote a breath-taking guitar part – gnarled, twisted, winding and almost Eastern in flavour, it utterly transformed the song and turned it into a slinky, prowling beast that melted into a terrifying maelstrom of raging noise. I seem to remember Bernard and I writing 'Moving' and 'Pantomime Horse' on the same day, or certainly very close together. 'Moving' was a fantastic live song that was eventually ruined in the studio by horrible production, but at its heart is a pulsing, pounding rant inspired by being wrenched out of one life and stuffed into a new one. I've always enjoyed playing around with homophones and loved the double meaning of the title. The word 'lassoing' in the lyrics comes from a moment when, flushed with a burgeoning confidence in my writing, I jokingly challenged Alan one evening to come up with an odd word for me to try to shoe-horn into the song, and that was it. You can sense Bernard's growing confidence too from the dynamics of the track: how he cleverly inverted the standard quiet/loud contemporary grunge dynamic into the opposite, making the verse frenetic, and the chorus open and spacious. It's a bitter regret for me that we were too naive in the studio to resist the temptation of adding horrible phasing to the track at that point, thereby rendering the album version weak and gimmicky. 'Pantomime Horse' is still one of the greatest ever Suede songs. When Bernard first played me the music it was in a different time signature, and I think my suggestion that we put it in 6/8 waltz time was inspired by The Smiths' 'That Joke Isn't Funny Anymore'. Anyway, it worked, and I set about writing a slightly self-piteous lyric that built to a wild, passionate denouement. The final scream of *'Have you ever tried it that way?'* is born from the torment of sexual jealousy but it's also intended as a probing, haranguing question about class and poverty and privilege.

I love 'To The Birds' – its looping, driving, almost Philip Glass-like guitar and bass intro, and the way it shifts and rises to its towering coda. It's a song about overcoming loss and loneliness with a sort of 'I Will Survive' motif, and is very much set against the backdrop of the break up, with me cast somewhat melodramatically as the abandoned troubadour perched on a balcony with just the pigeons as an audience. The colloquial connotation of the word 'birds' wasn't lost on me, but I have always loved juggling shades of meaning. For me so much of the lifeblood of a song is about subjective interpretation, without which it would be just dead, like a specimen under glass – a butterfly in a dusty case. I'm aware of the paradox as I sit here and share my memories of these tracks, but my own interpretation isn't absolute, merely a starting point. This may sound contradictory given my earlier tirade but, when it's intended in the right spirit, one of my favourite things is hearing other people's readings of them. So long as it doesn't feel gossipy or absolutist, it can be fun and creative and keeps the music breathing, and I never feel qualified enough to contradict it.

The strange thing is, while we were writing all these new songs, Justine was still in the band and performing them with us. It should have felt like some sort of twisted victory, but it didn't. The whole situation was becoming increasingly untenable; a strange blend of growing excitement but palpable tension as I tried to reconcile and balance the thrill of a creative awakening with the awkward, shuffling banalities of still working together. There was a period of about six months where we were still playing depressing pub gigs with her to a handful of uninterested people. The difference was that the material was now becoming incendiary even if the response wasn't. Often there would still be more people on stage than in the audience. At one particular show at The Amersham Arms, New Cross, we played to a single person: Simon's cousin Paul. Looking back it seems ludicrous, as by that point the set was boasting 'The Drowners', 'To The Birds', 'He's Dead' and 'Moving'. Any A&R men who did happen upon us, and who hadn't already seen us when we were shit and passed, were probably looking for the new Ride or Chapterhouse and couldn't see how our increasingly dramatic, edgy energy sat comfortably with the flavour of the month. We made a demo at a cheap East London studio called Rocking Horse; simple, exciting versions of 'The Drowners', 'He's Dead', 'Moving' and 'To The Birds'. The same music industry that would greet those same songs with flowery, lavish plaudits a year or so later gave a collective disinterested shrug and turned away to look for the new Slowdive. By this point, even though we were seething with frustration, our self-belief was becoming hardened by a flinty sense of determination, and so we gritted our teeth knowing that one day, one day, the moment would come.

Playing this clutch of new songs with Justine still hammering away on her rhythm guitar was becoming increasingly wrong. Apart from the obvious strain related to being in a band fronted by her ex-boyfriend, she was also becoming much more opinionated and itching with questions about where we were going artistically, creating real friction and schisms between her and the rest of us. She loved the punchier, punkier stuff but began to despise 'To The Birds' and 'Pantomime Horse' and all the grander, more epic material, partly because she had a different vision for the band but also, I think, because she sensed that they contained bitter, barbed stabs at her. And so the tension mounted. It came to a head finally; in a heated exchange after rehearsal one night she told me she didn't like those songs, and I replied that 'Pantomime Horse' and 'To The Birds' were exactly the kind of things that I wanted to write and if she didn't like them then she was in the wrong band. A few days later, after yet another empty, loveless show — this time at ULU in Malet Street — she finally decided that she'd had enough, putting her Rickenbacker in the back of the Renault and disappearing into the night for the last time; driving off to a new life and exiting mine for many years.

10

With Justine gone, the band got better. I don't mean to sound harsh or cruel but suddenly there was a clarity that we hadn't had before, as purely sonically her rough rhythm guitar-playing had cluttered and muddied the sound. Free of this, Bernard was forced to play fuller, chunkier parts in a heavier style that suited the violent, belligerent edge that the band was developing live. I think she would be the first to agree that her exit played a huge role in our later success and, of course, in hers. Personally, her absence allowed me to let go of her in a way I just hadn't been able to before, and now I had left college her once consuming, looming ubiquity was reduced to a memory; painful, yes, but without the confusion and hesitation and tension of her presence. Now Bernard and I were free to write how we wrote best – instinctively – and the next couple of years would yield our best ever work. The feeling in the band was much more one of unity as we went about our business, the four of us able to bond and gel in a way that we never could previously. And like any half-decent band we became a little gang: fiercely loyal and protective of each other, borrowing each other's clothes and finishing each other's sentences. We cancelled all of our upcoming gigs and withdrew from our non-existent audience, spending months just writing and rehearsing. Holed up on Hackney Road, wreathed in cigarette smoke and with endless cups of tea cooling on the window ledges and on the amps, we slowly became the band that the public would first know as Suede, emerging from our cocoon, blinking in the daylight. We had a rehearsal booked at the Premises one evening, and both Mat and Simon were ill or couldn't make it or something. Bernard and I didn't cancel it, and turned up to try to write something. He was jamming away with a spidery arpeggio piece and I just started singing, and magically, almost like the 'Light My Fire' scene in *The Doors* film, by the end of the evening we had written 'My Insatiable One'. Like everything I was writing at that time it was massively coloured by heartbreak, but this time I was writing about myself in the third person and from Justine's point of view; fictionalising a situation where she was regretting her choices and where the 'he' in the lyrics was actually me. I found this shift in perspective really thrilling as a writer and it suddenly opened up enormous vistas, which I began to explore through other songs in that early period, looking at the world through the eyes of housewives and gay men and lonely dads. Dylan had done it in my favourite ever song of his, 'North Country Blues', where he inhabited the persona of a nineteenth-century miner's wife, and I thought it was a fascinating, exciting device. Sadly, a year or so later, when we had become shrouded in notoriety and success, some would choose to see it as social tourism. Given the levels of real, cynical, social tourism during that decade, when groups of patronising middle-class boys were making money by aping the accents and culture of the working classes, the irony would be exquisite.

But the songs kept flowing. Now that he was the sole guitarist Bernard began to fill the songs with more primal parts. He once told me that, bizarrely, he was inspired by the rhythm of Cher's 'The Shoop Shoop Song' after hearing it on the radio and came up with the thrilling, primitive, pounding groove of what was to become 'Metal Mickey'. I don't really remember writing my part to this – it probably came together in the rehearsal room where I would invent melodies and sketch rough lyrics, screened by the squeal of feedback and blankets of noise as the band thrashed away. I bought myself a cheap Sony voice recorder that I would constantly be whispering ideas into. Mat once called me 'the worst traffic hazard in west London' as I'd stumble blindly into busy roads muttering and warbling into my Dictaphone, oblivious to the choruses of angry horns and screeching brakes. The lyrics to 'Metal Mickey' were a little throwaway to be frank, but it suited the music's joyous, teenage rush. If I'm honest they were partly an homage to the only contemporary band I had any time for – Daisy Chainsaw – who had a kind of thrilling scruffy glamour of their own. The song was very much set in the grubby, seedy world of the early nineties London indie circuit: the plastic pint glasses, the depressing pub gigs, the furtive shuffling failure. Using my dole money I'd buy cigarettes, cat food, rice and vegetables from Portobello Market, and if there was anything left I'd go to the Oxfam or Sue Ryder charity shops and pick up second-hand clothes. As Mr Lydon once so brilliantly put it 'clothes are so important in an unimportant way' and I loved the old seventies shirts and little leather bomber jackets you could get for a few pounds. As well as the fact that they were cheap it appealed to me that these were the kind of clothes that no one wore any more, and soon by a process of osmosis and expedience the rest of the band started borrowing my things or wearing similar stuff. When we eventually achieved success and started penetrating beyond the music press into fashion magazines, those people thought it was a stylised 'look' that we had decided upon – some sort of kitsch, ironic comment. I took great pleasure in laughingly telling them it was actually because we were very, very poor. Mat later summed it up nicely by saying that 'we'd all cleaned toilets for a living'.

Sorry to disappoint anyone who thought otherwise, but I have never felt any particular kinship with any other band, any of our 'contemporaries'. When people look back on the decade I expect they imagine us skipping merrily down Camden High Street as part of some sort of jolly little clique, but we were never part of the ugly, beery cartoon that defined the latter half of the decade. And thank god for that. I saw our absence as I saw absence from any elite: as a wonderful, freeing thing. But in that nascent state, when we were feeling around for a sense of who we were, it felt like we were completely on our own; like explorers cutting a path through the forest with machetes and pith helmets. The feeling of 'Britishness' that we were developing in our words and in our music and in our style was something exciting that we felt we had almost stumbled upon, and as such it felt brave and raw and beautifully out of step. Obviously, it had bled through to us through a procession of acts from the past, but in 1991, when all the other bands who later went on to try to claim it as theirs were still locked into a miserable mess of shoegazing and baggy, it felt like it was utterly ours and ours alone. But there was a huge difference between what I was trying to do with my writing and what those who came later did. I was never celebrating Britishness – I was documenting it.

The point was to reflect the world that I saw around me and that world just happened to be Britain: a cheapened, failed world that had nothing to do with the laddish, jingoistic and frankly patronising inter-pretation that would follow. It had always frustrated me that so many song lyrics were simply what I call 'rock speak', clichés borrowed from Jimi Hendrix, Jim Morrison et al, meaningless drivel about 'elevating one's soul' etc. etc. I wanted to use my own voice and sing in my accent about my world, broken and drab and scruffy and strange though it was, and try to do it with some sense of grace and poetry. Looking back over that decade, it now feels that the thing that we gave birth to in those grimy east London rehearsal rooms in 1990 and 1991 ultimately betrayed us, and like the child that a mother finds stealing from her purse we would never be able to look at it in quite the same way again.

At some point around this time, Simon came out to us. He quietly said it in public while we were having a drink after rehearsal, and heartbreakingly I didn't hear him at first as Alan had to mention it to me later that evening. I've always admired Simon's quiet dignity, and his shyness and concern about how we would take the news just made him seem even more decent. As soon as I was told, I immediately called him and put him at ease that it didn't make the slightest bit of difference to anything. Why would it? But even in the liberal nineties the ugly seeds of homophobia were still ripening, and I suppose he was anxious despite the fact that the lyrics to the songs were probably starting to bleed through to him and he was hopefully beginning to feel part of something that was documenting the marginal and the put-upon. Maybe this was my attempt to give a voice to those on the fringes of acceptance, as in a way it artic-ulated how I saw my place in life. It was sad that what was intended as an inclusive approach would be later seen as 'fake' and 'opportunistic', but I have learned that with some issues it's almost impossible to adopt a position of any subtlety.

Money might not be able to buy you happiness, but a lack of it can make life fucking miserable and London can be particularly brutal if you're poor. The grinding poverty of bread-line dole life in John Major's Britain was becoming unbearable so I felt it was time to start to apply for jobs. At first, it would be for lofty positions that I had no experience in or qualifications for, until the tide of snooty rejections made me gradually lower my sights and eventually I ended up looking for work in shops. It felt like I was always either under- or over-qualified, and during a six-month period of constant applications I received one single invitation for an interview at a stationers in Bond Street. The subsequent rejection from them made me finally accept my state of penury and I gave up looking for paid work, but still I needed to do something to fill those endless, empty, drifting afternoons when we weren't writing or rehearsing. From somewhere or other I'd heard about a community centre in Highgate called Lauderdale House, nestled on the edge of Waterlow Park just off the top of the Archway Road. I marched up there one wintery day and hustled and nagged until they agreed to let me help out and do some voluntary work. I started doing shifts lifting things and making tea and manning the reception desk, directing people to literature workshops and yoga classes and drop-in centres. I loved the warmth and sense of community, and became very fond of Highgate, an enclave strangely separate from the rest of London and appropriately excluded from my old *A–Z*. Secluded, mildly eccentric and almost anachronistic, it was an area that I'd return to for a while in 1994 to write my parts for *Dog Man Star*. Day after day I would deal with young mums and lonely wives whose mascara-streaked faces betrayed a back story of hardship and frustration and broken nights. Their plight somehow resonated with me, and one day during my lunch break I took my cheese and pickle sandwich and my notebook out to a bench on Waterlow Park, and wrote what would become the lyrics to 'Sleeping Pills'. The song was never the melodramatic plea against suicide that it was often interpreted as. It was just an anthem for the Valium housewives killing time and softly numbing themselves to make it through another day. This was something I strongly identified with – my own days often stretching out before me, vacant and endless and overwhelming, while I stared at the hands of the clock and waited for something to happen. Indeed, I think the only reason that writing from a shifted perspective worked for me was because I felt there was always a strong sense of empathy; it was never as simple and unsophisticated as just straight-forward characterisation because the vignettes contained fragments and emotions from my own life. 'Write about what you know,' they say, and I always did. When Bernard played me a graceful, ebbing guitar piece he had written that winded and built to a stormy crescendo, I knew my characters had found their home, and I would return to the theme on two key songs on the next album: 'Still Life' and 'The 2 Of Us'.

Our cocooned period of growth and exile over, we started sniffing around for gigs again. By this point we had been approached by one John Eydmann, a sweet, soft man, now sadly dead, whose cartoon puppy-dog eyes always reminded me of Droopy or a young Tom Hulce. He had worked for Fire records and had come across us on the bottom rungs of the circuit and offered to help out. His position even within the lower reaches of the business gave us some tangible feeling of connection, a glimpse of the possibility of progress and a vague promise of traction, so we accepted his offer to manage us. He was destined to guide us away from long drunken journeys rattling around in the back of smoky, dark Transit vans to meetings with major label moguls in Manhattan skyscrapers and Malibu Beach mansions. But for now we were still firmly earthbound, a band with a steely ambition and a growing arsenal of incendiary songs, and yet without anything approaching even a murmur of success. After a couple of shows that trod the old, familiar, depressing spiral of underachievement, John booked us a gig at The Camden Falcon, in a draughty dark room at the back of a pub that was a mainstay of the London indie circuit in the early nineties; a grubby haunt for low-level emerging bands and inscrutable journalists. We had played there a few months before with Justine to a thin audience that included the singer Momus, a kind of minor hero of mine at the time, who had enthralled me with his cold, detached, sexual imagery and Brel-like paeans to indecency. Justine had met him at a party and he must have become enamoured as the video he shot of the gig that somehow made it back to us was almost exclusively close-ups of her breasts. Anyway, the gig that John organised was billed as our 'Christmas Show'. The bitter irony of this forced, fake jollity would soon make itself apparent. The audience consisted entirely of two people: John and his girlfriend, Fiona. It was a freezing December night and the lack of any crowd or body heat resulted in a perishing chill. My abiding memory is of each member of the band taking it in turns to press himself up against the wall-mounted radiator at the back of the stage as we bleakly and pointlessly ran through our set.

It was around this time that we were starting to need help driving and shifting our gear around, so John introduced us to someone who could help out. His name was Charlie Charlton, a warm, lovable Teessider, who at the time had bizarre, early nineties Back to the Planet-style dreadlocks that made him look like a cartoon ant. Charlie was the sort of tirelessly helpful and capable person that everyone secretly wants to be their dad and, indeed, we came to trust him and rely on him so much that we would later appoint him our manager, and he would guide us through the first flush of real success and towards the heights of the first two albums and beyond.

Looking back we must have been developing some sort of nascent, stuttering momentum, but it still felt like we were locked firmly outside the sweet-shop. Then, late in the winter of 1991, something surprising happened – we were invited to play at the *NME*'s 'On For '92' event, a showcase for emerging bands. The 'On For . . .' gigs were a bit of an institution at a time when the influence and reach of the *NME* was paramount and their approval utterly essential for virtually any success within alternative circles. We tumbled into the fantasy that this could be the chance we had been waiting for: the fabled 'big break', exposure for the songs we were becoming so proud of, and maybe an escape hatch into something other than dole queues and dreary poverty. We trudged over to The Venue in New Cross one bleak January afternoon to take our sound-check slot and then shuffled off to some cheap nearby cafe to drink tea and eat salad kebabs and anxiously await the evening. We were sandwiched in third place on a four-band bill between Adorable, Midway Still and a band called Fabulous. The show was fairly unremarkable other than that unusually for us there were more people in the audience than on the stage. We played most of the new jewels in our grow-ing repertoire: 'Pantomime Horse', 'The Drowners', 'Metal Mickey', 'Moving' and probably closing with 'To The Birds'. In those early days and indeed until much later, when people had actually paid to specifi-cally come to see us we only ever played about six or seven songs, mainly because we simply didn't have more, but also as a kind of manifesto of arrogance, always favouring the thrilling punch of brevity over the workmanlike, over the dull, over the dutiful.

After the last song we would throw down our instruments in a kind of petulant rage and storm off, never returning for an encore, considering them fake and 'showbizzy'. Most of the column inches in the *NME* the following week were devoted to Fabulous, whose journalist singer knew much better how to work the cameras. Our mention was really a footnote, but it was positive and contained an undertone of intrigue. The tide of record company offers didn't arrive, but we were approached by one man who had seen us that evening and heard our demo. His name was Saul Galpern: a shrewd and passionate Scotsman, who looked a little like the footballer Andy Gray, and who was just beginning to establish a small independent label called Nude Records. Later, he would become a mentor and a friend and a key part of the tale but for now he was just another bloke to be suspicious of. He called me at my flat and we had a slightly odd, prickly conversation, but despite the awkwardness I could tell that he really got the songs and that he could see in them what the rest of the business still couldn't, and I suppose you could say he began to court us.

It's interesting for me to see how the momentum of the story shifts at this point. Reading back I can see how my early life was in a state of stasis almost, and so I was forced to confront the microscopic detail of my odd little world simply because that's all that I had. The beautiful curiosity one has as a child inevitably and sadly dissolves as the paths open up and you succumb to the pace of adult life. Whereas my early life was a broad tapestry of detailed close-ups, all I remember about these mid-stages is a series of early career milestones, so it's hard not to make the story run away with itself as it moves from a descriptive piece to something more plot-driven. 'Real' life had somehow become irrelevant: I wasn't reading newspapers or watching TV or doing anything that wasn't connected to the band at this juncture. It had become utterly, utterly all-consuming, and to be honest that's the only way to approach it; to dive into it head first and drown in its savage tide. Even my private life by this point was starting to feel like a mere vehicle to generate songs as I willingly exposed myself to increasingly bizarre and frictional personal dramas and extreme situations, knowing that somehow the prize seemed worth the sacrifice. It was almost as if my life was starting to belong to someone else as I began to see it as some curious experiment in song writing. Slowly a persona was taking grip of me, and it would only be many years later that I would be able to begin the quiet, private process of redressing that. But one's twenties are a magical time; they have a habit of defining you and I have few regrets.

The modest seeds of rumour sown by our presence at the show in New Cross must have created gentle ripples amongst the London music-biz taste-makers because almost imperceptibly things began to shift: the planets began to align and people started to mutter and heads finally, finally started to turn. Here was the gear change heralding the first thrilling breath of success that had previously seemed so beyond us. The not fitting in that had always been so frustrating and caused so many people to pass us over or ignore us had finally become our strength, and there was a real sense that we were doing something completely on our own, something special, something unique: fresh and unfamiliar and tinged with the shock of the new. The overt Englishness, the quirky realism and the fumbling, scruffy sexuality which had previously put people off was now delivered with élan and confidence, wonderfully against the grain and thrillingly exciting. I'd always wanted the band to inhabit its own universe, a 'Suede World', and as our skill as performers and song-writers evolved this world began to resonate and speak to people and reveal itself to them. And as the song-writing began to embrace a lustful, lurching tone so in parallel we as a band started to throw off our self-consciousness, becoming grinding and aggressive and primal, flaunting ourselves and the immense passion we felt for the music we were making. Simon's powerful angry drumming, and Bernard and Mat's increasingly uninhibited playing became a sort of throbbing motor that unlocked the dark heart of the songs. And suddenly there were people in the audience who we actually didn't know: people who had begun to seek us out and, shockingly, who had actually paid for the privilege. The dreaded D-shaped space in front of me began to fill with sweaty, human form, magically unfamiliar, and clammy with passion and curiosity. Gradually, it all became more fevered, and though by this point we certainly hadn't yet achieved full scale 'Suede-mania', there was still a sense that, to again borrow one of Lydon's excellent phrases, they might, just possibly, 'lovingly tear me apart'. We played another show at the Underworld in Camden, and the following Tuesday, when I made my usual trip down to Tottenham Court Road tube station to buy the inkies, a glowing review leapt out of the *Melody Maker* describing us as a 'snarling, prowling rock beast'. It seemed that a wonderful tipping point had been reached. Our next show was yet another at the Falcon, but a country mile away from the cruel pantomime we had endured there in December. This time, the palpable frisson and murmur of excitement in the crowd wasn't just because Morrissey, Suggs and Kirsty MacColl had turned up to see us, it was because at last we had something that people seemed to want. John Mulvey's breathless, excitable review that appeared in the *NME* the following week was our first real taste of press approval, and after years of struggle against indifference and disinterest it was so, so sweet. And this thing that people started to want, as they suddenly massed and swarmed like flying ants, if I could be allowed a brief moment of flowery indulgence, seemed like something special. It was ours and ours alone – our ragged hymn, our howl of frustration – a poem to failure and loss and a paean to the cheapened, indifferent Britain that we saw before us. And as we stabbed and kicked against the dreary mediocrity of the time we did it with a style, a spirit and a force that ended up breaking down doors and laying the foundations for the music that defined a decade.

Saul continued to court and flatter, and I think we all secretly loved his rambunctious passion, so one day in February we found ourselves marching up to his offices on Langham Street and finally putting pen to paper. I don't remember much about actually signing – I was probably late and everyone else was probably anxious – but we finally did it, and when at last we tumbled back down the stairs and on to the pavements of Fitzrovia, our future was set, and London stretched out before us, beautiful and plain in the weak winter sun.

To buy any of our books and to find out
more about Abacus and Little, Brown, our authors
and titles, as well as events and book clubs,
visit our website

www.littlebrown.co.uk

and follow us on Twitter

**@AbacusBooks
@LittleBrownUK**